SUBMISSION
Is For Husbands, Too

Mark R. Littleton

ACCENT BOOKS
Denver, CO 80215

Contents

ACCENT BOOKS

A division of Accent Publications, Inc.
12100 West Sixth Avenue
P.O. Box 15337
Denver, Colorado 80215

Printed in the United States of America

Library of Congress Catalog Card Number 87-71221

ISBN 0-89636-239-6

To
the many couples
who have encouraged, nurtured,
challenged, loved, and set an example
for my wife, Valerie, and me.
We thank you
and love you.

Introduction
This Book Is For Husbands *and* Wives

When a letter from the editor at Accent Books arrived in my mailbox many months ago, my only previous contact with the publisher was from leafing through some of their books on the shelves of the local bookstores. When they suggested that I consider doing a book on submission in marriage, I didn't hesitate to put together a formal outline. I was excited. But I had no idea what I was getting into—both from the writing and the marital standpoint.

This book has forced me to re-evaluate much of my thinking about marriage, submission to Christ, and what it means to love my wife as Christ loved the church. I began to realize how little I understood what our Lord created when He created the marital bond.

What I offer here is a biblical look at the issue of a husband's submission to Christ. I have provided numerous examples from my own life and marriage. More importantly, I have tried to analyze, in depth, what Scripture says. The result is something my wife and I are striving to achieve.

But it's difficult.

When I first became a Christian, walking with Jesus was a dream come true—strawberries and cream all the way. But as I've grown, it seems I have become more and more aware of my own inherent selfishness, self-absorption, self-orientation, and self-love. Many leaders today speak about self-image and the need to love yourself. I have no problem with loving myself. Sure, I get frustrated with myself. Sure, I put myself down now and then. But when it comes to paydirt, it is usually "me" first, even though I may try to present a different image. Thanks to our sin nature, selfishness is as ingrained in us as thirst for water or hunger for bread. It is a problem we all battle. It is the most basic of all sins.

I confess that I struggle with the issues raised in this book. Just the same, I am seeing progress. The joy of walking with Christ is that He accepts you where you are and works step by step, day by day to lead you closer to Him. In that is tremendous hope.

Wives may read this book and come away determined that their husbands will start living up to the Scriptures. They will put a copy in their husband's lunchbox, on his nightstand, or in his sock drawer. More than likely, he'll check the title and snort, "*Submission?* For men? Come on! That's ridiculous. I'd no sooner submit to my wife than I would to my teenaged daughter."

Or, "Look, I'm the head of my home. That settles it, and I'm not reading it."

Or, "The author's a lunatic. And possibly a heretic!"

Or, "Why, this way the world would end up being run by women. What kind of place would that be?"

Nonetheless, I hope your response will be something more like, "Really, Lord? Help me to begin living up to these standards and ideals you've given us."

Submission for husbands does not mean a sudden termination of authority, position, or headship. It does not mean that we let our wives navigate for the family. Rather, it is something far greater and better than most of us could imagine.

I hope these pages inspire you with the real meaning of biblical submission so that you see it in all of its beauty and perfection. For many, submission has a bad connotation. It seems to legitimize such things as the husband as dictator and the wife as doormat. Yet, nothing could be further from God's truth.

I'd like to explode those myths and expose you to some of the most liberating truths a husband and wife can find. Come with me as we explore these possibilities.

SECTION ONE:
A Foundation To Build On

—1—

Submission Is for Husbands, Too!

Tom edged into my office and said, "Can we talk about some things?"

"Sure," I said, motioning for him to sit down.

He was uncomfortable at first, but slowly he began telling me about his home situation. "I've moved out several times. But this time I think we've really had it. I want us to stay married, but we just can't seem to change."

"What specifically is the problem?"

"It's just that she wants me around all the time. If I stop on the way home from work to spend some time with my friends, she's angry that I didn't call her. If I want to go off for a weekend camping, she doesn't understand. She gave up most of her friends when we got married. But now she expects me to give up everything and everyone for her. My self-image is shot. I have no confidence. I've even lied to her. And I don't feel good about that. But I don't know what to do."

I gazed at Tom's dejected face. I was certain the first thing that had to be done was lead him to Christ.

But something else rang deep within my soul. It seemed to me that Tom was butting his mind and his feelings against one of the most fundamental aspects of marriage: the mutual submission of each mate to the other. He seemed to think that although he was married, nothing had changed. He could still operate as though he was not married. He wanted to hang out with the boys and not have to answer to anyone about it. He was determined to "do his own thing" regardless of his wife's feelings. It was tearing him and his wife apart.

It was an important insight for me because I had been thinking a lot about submission at that time. I had always thought submission was largely for wives. But as I studied Scripture, I began to see it was also for husbands.

Peter and Paul Spelled It Out

When I say "mutual submission," I am talking about something very different from the submission of the wife to the husband's leadership. Scripture is clear in such passages as Colossians 3:18, Ephesians 5:22-24, and I Corinthians 11:3 that the wife is to be submissive to her husband. That is, she is under his authority. As the marriage vows say, she is to love and honor him.

But Scripture also speaks of another aspect of submission, the mutual submission of all believers to Christ and one another.

Both Peter and Paul explain this truth. Paul reveals the idea in Ephesians 5. After commanding us to be filled with the Spirit, he illustrates how we can know when we are filled: by sharing the Word, singing, being grateful, and submitting. He says, "Be subject to one another in the fear of Christ" (Ephesians 5:21, NASB).

Even though the English uses the word "subject" instead of "submit," both words translate the single Greek term, *hupotasso.* It is a military word which means to "put oneself under" or to "recognize and obey the authority" of another. Paul is saying that we are to willingly put others ahead of ourselves in all Christian relationships. Philippians 2:3-4 is helpful. "Do nothing from selfishness or empty conceit, but with humility of mind let each of you regard one another as more important than himself; do not merely look out for your own personal interests, but also for the interests of others."

Notice that Paul says in Ephesians that we are to do this "in the fear of Christ." It is something we do out of reverence, respect, and love for Jesus.

How many of us go through the day in this frame of mind? Just starting off in the morning I begin with concern about myself. First, there is getting up. For whom did I set that alarm? Whose teeth am I brushing? The hair I am combing so carefully—that isn't my wife's, is it? That shirt I'm selecting—isn't that for *me,* for *my* body?

And what about the rest of the day? At the office I'm doing *my* paperwork, not someone else's. (Though it often seems like I'm doing everyone's but my own.) I am copying the things *I* need to copy. I input into the computer the things *I* am working with, not my secretary's.

At lunchtime I consume *my* sandwich. When I drive home, it's back to the offensive stance. Pass this guy. Cut off that one. Speed up through this light. Slow down now—that fellow ahead isn't paying attention. He's swerving right into *my* lane!

Every day our passion is for ourselves. But Paul is introducing a whole new concept, a revolutionary attitude—look out for number two! And three. And four.

And Paul does not leave it there. This is where he jumps right into the fray and zeroes in on wives. (How like a man!) He goes on to say the way a wife is to be submissive is by responding to her husband as though he were the Lord Himself (Ephesians 5:23-25). Imagine that! Treating your mate like he was Jesus Himself? We have all heard of wives who treat their husbands like kings. But this does seem a little much.

Yet, Paul makes it very sensible. He gives the illustration of the church's relationship to Christ. Just like the church is subject to Jesus, so a wife should be to her husband. A husband is subject to the leadership and example of Christ. A wife places herself under her husband's authority. She follows his lead.

Paul does not stop there, though. He has a lot more to say to the husband. A husband is to be submissive by loving his wife and sacrificing himself for her like Christ did for the church (Ephesians 5:25-33).

Now that *is* tough. Maybe a wife has to be subject to her husband in everything, but a husband has to literally sacrifice his life for her!

Still, this isn't so unfamiliar. It's the basic principle of Scripture. "Love your neighbor as yourself." "However you want others to treat you, so treat them." "The Lord laid down His life for us; we ought to lay down our lives for one another" (John 15:12-13; Matthew 22:37-39,7:12). It's the only way Christianity operates—on a principle of unconditional, sacrificial love and giving.

"But it's so idealistic."

Absolutely.

And realistic.

Think about it. What if people did practice this principle, just in the context of the home? What kind of homes would we have? Probably, precisely the kind for which we long.

Still, practicing this principle does not mean subservience or becoming someone's doormat or slave. Rather, it means consciously putting others in a position of higher priority than ourselves. Who occupies the highest priority in our minds? Whose needs are met the fastest when they arise? Usually, they are our own. But submission tears us out of that mindset and forces us to consider others, to put ourselves in others' situations, and to treat them as we would be treated.

It is difficult to do. Many times I fail miserably. But it is necessary for the survival of any real relationship. And it is possible for it to become a character trait of your life.

An Amplification

Peter amplifies the concept of submission even more potently in I Peter 2:11—3:8. The husband's submission is to the Lord and to His principles. This works out in the context of marriage as a submission to basic truths regarding his relationship with his wife. She is not the only one who puts herself under authority. While she submits to her husband, He is to put himself under the Lord and do what is best for his wife.

Look, for example, at the role of a democratic president in contrast to a dictator. A dictator does what he wants to satisfy his own whims and to meet his own needs. Whether it is good for anyone else does not matter. What matters is that he wants it. But an elected president is expected to consider the needs of his electorate first. If he does not, he will soon be cast out of office.

Similarly, the submissive husband sees himself as a president, not a dictator. He puts the concerns and desires of his wife ahead of his own in making decisions. He seeks to accomplish what is best for all.

In Peter's letter, we find four statements about submission that are critical to the life of a marriage. These are universal principles that every Christian should practice, but let's apply them in this context to husbands. In fact, I have been challenged to practice these in my relationship with my wife, Valerie. They have deepened and strengthened our marriage as never before.

Doing What's Right—Regardless

Peter draws out the first principle in I Peter 2:12. He tells us to keep our behavior excellent among our neighbors so that if they slander us as evildoers, they will begin to notice our good deeds and ultimately glorify God.

In 2:13-15 he says the same thing in relation to the government: we are to do right and silence foolish men.

Then, he reminds servants in 2:18, "Be submissive to your masters with all respect, not only to those who are good and gentle, but also to those who are unreasonable."

And in 3:1-2, wives are told to be submissive to disobedient husbands so that their husbands may be won by their godly behavior.

When Peter arrives at 3:7 for his instructions to husbands, he has the idea of submission entrenched in his mind. He says, "You husbands likewise . . . ."

That has become an important principle for me, not because my wife is disobedient, but because it has taught me that I am responsible for my own reactions, words, thoughts, and deeds regardless of hers. Husbands are to *do what's right even though our wives (or anyone else) may not.*

This has helped us, for instance, in the context of a disagreement. Occasionally we will come to words about something. In the past, when I did not get my way, I would begin throwing out hot words, reminding Val of past infractions, or simply stomp off into the sunset. It did not matter who or what started it. Things would escalate until I would start pitching every curve I could. My anger stoked hers, and vice versa.

I remember several situations where, when Val disagreed with me, I would stomp into the bedroom, slam the door, and resolve not to speak to her for three hours. But the Lord would remind me, "Be angry and yet do not sin." Sometimes I would argue, but ultimately He would win. In a few moments I would choose to make an apology, and we would be hugging. The still small voice seemed to quip, "Now wasn't that better than three hours of silence?"

This principle of submission has helped me to avoid the "slam-the-door-and-stomp-around" treatment. When we disagree, I do not have to respond with anger. I can listen and not take it personally. The result is that we have learned to disagree without cutting, wounding, or maiming one another verbally.

It has been a difficult lesson, though, and it remains difficult. The question the Lord always asks is, "Will you obey *me* or the feelings of the moment?" He has been helping us to learn to do the former in all areas.

This first element of submission is critical. If we are not

willing to obey the Lord's Word regardless of the actions of others, we are not really obeying at all. We are making our obedience contingent on others' behavior. This destroys the whole power of submission.

Putting Her Needs First

This leads to a second thought Peter draws out: *submission is putting your wife's needs ahead of your own.*

This again comes in the context of Peter's previous words on submission. He says of our relationships that we are to "Honor all men; love the brotherhood, fear God, honor the king" (2:17). After that, he speaks of Jesus who "suffered for you, leaving you an example for you to follow in His steps" (2:21). In each case, personal desires and needs are put after another's.

This has been another pivotal principle for our marriage. I have seen it work especially in the area of listening. Every now and then when Val and I are sitting on the couch, I will overhear her begin to carry on a conversation with herself. " 'So how was your day, honey?' 'Oh, fine. The baby was feeling bad, but we got along.' 'Well, I'm sorry to hear that. Is she better?' 'I think so. But she does require a lot of attention. Not like a wife does, you know . . . .' " I put down the paper and say, "Okay, okay, what do you want to talk about?"

There are other times when I am dead tired, barely able to hobble to the sack, but she has things troubling her. That is prime time for putting her needs ahead of my own. Sometimes I will say, "Can it wait? I'm dead, Hon." And she will put it on hold. But there are other times when I must sacrifice a few extra minutes of sleep for her sanity.

It is also true that your wife often needs some extra shots of affection. To have to ask for a hug somehow destroys the power of it. We men tend to downplay such things. But after hearing Valerie's feelings on the issue, I decided to take more time to show affection with spontaneous one-minute hugs and friendly caresses.

Dr. Howard Hendricks gave his students at Dallas Theological Seminary an excellent marital concept with his "leaving his briefcase by the road routine." He told us that at a certain point, while driving home from work, he would mentally drop his briefcase and its contents by the side of the road. From that point on, he thought about nothing but his family, wife, and what he would be doing at home that evening. I decided to try it in our marriage. The result has been that I have begun to think more about her and my family's needs and how I am going to meet them that evening. This has brought new and refreshing creativity into my displays of affection as well as enabling me to discover new ways of helping out around our home.

There are so many ways a husband can do this, from offering to wash the dishes, clean up the car, and help with the cooking, to meditating on and anticipating a wife's deeper needs of fellowship, understanding, and honor. Some men sneer at such things as the first, saying it is women's work. Or the wife should get those things done before he gets home. And they never quite get to the second, intangible investment. But is the home the sole responsibility of the wife? How would the husband fare if he were cooped up all day with a three-year-old and no one to talk to but the dishwasher and the toaster? It is more a matter of attitude than anything else. Once a husband decides he is going to give her needs priority, the Spirit will guide him in working it out daily.

This principle again is a universal. But applied to the husband and his relationship with his wife, it is critical.

Will you put her needs first? Or keep your own paramount and frustrate both of you?

Entrust Your Own Needs To God

In this context, though, one might legitimately ask, "What about my own needs? When do they get met?" Once again Peter offers help: *submission is the ability to entrust your own needs to God.*

Peter illustrates this from Jesus' life. When He was reviled, ridiculed, beaten, and murdered, He didn't respond in kind, but "kept entrusting Himself to Him who judges righteously" (2:23).

I have found, likewise, that there are many occasions in marriage when a husband must put his needs on hold. But that does not mean they won't be met. I find that if I turn to God and say, "Lord, you know my needs. You meet them. I'll leave them in your care," the Lord always does what is right.

Almost four years ago, while I was serving as a pastor, my wife and I went through a terrible church situation that led to my resignation. Throughout the period, both my wife and I were attacked and put-down. When we finally left the pastorate, she was certain she never wanted to embark on another ministry. I decided to seek secular work. However, my heart was in the ministry, and I knew I would not feel comfortable without returning sometime. But Val was hurting also, and I didn't want to put any pressure on her.

My tendency is to debate and argue an issue until my opponent finally agrees with me. But then I discovered this principle from Peter. As a result, I left the question of returning to the ministry in God's hands. I prayed, "Lord, if you want me to get back into it, you convince Val. I'm not talking her into it." The result has been that she decided on her own that she wants me to get back into full-time work for the Lord if that is what I desire. I never brought the subject up (although she did frequently). The Lord was working to meet both our needs.

Now I can entrust just about everything about my wife to the Lord—any changes I think she should make, her growth, needs, strengths, in fact, our whole relationship. God is able. He will make it turn out not only for the good, but for the best. Even though, like most people, I have not always found patience easy.

On another occasion, I had a tremendous writing load and really needed to go into work on a Saturday. But I had already volunteered to take care of our daughter. I said, "Lord, it's in your hands. Whatever comes I'll accept it."

That morning Val called her mom who suggested they take Nicole and go out to buy her an Easter dress. Val said to me, "You can have the day to yourself. How's that?"

I was amazed. God knew my needs and engineered the meeting of them. I didn't have to manipulate, cajole or break my promise.

A husband who ceases to sneak, argue, challenge, and fight, but entrusts his needs to the Lord, will find a greater blessing than he could imagine. His marriage will become an adventure just to see how God will work things out.

Beware, though. Just because you put your needs in God's hands does not mean He will automatically do what you want. Sometimes He will meet them in a way wholly different from what you desire.

God Will Reward You

Still, Peter isn't done. Sometimes a husband is caught in a bad situation where these other principles of submission do not produce the right result. Some men remain patient, but their wives let the house fall apart. He controls his temper, but she insults him and nags him anyway. He works at being gentle, but she still does not respond to his caresses and kindness. What does he do?

This is where Peter's fourth thought about submission is helpful. He reveals that submission is *looking to God for your reward for obedience.* He says in 2:19, "For this finds favor, if for the sake of conscience toward God a man bears up under sorrows while suffering unjustly." Clearly, Peter proposes that obedience finds favor, and therefore a reward, from God.

I find that if I begin keeping tabs for every kindness or act of obedience, expecting that God will provide an immediate return on my investment, I am never satisfied. But if I look to God for my ultimate reward, then I am set free to obey the Word regardless of my wife's response.

Fortunately, my wife is highly responsive to the Lord and continually seeks to grow in grace. But this principle has struck me especially in the little things of marriage. I am learning to perform acts of love which my wife may never know about and which I promptly forget. But God doesn't.

For instance, one morning after a shower I dropped a towel on the floor of the bathroom and left it there, thinking, "It'll get picked up." But the still, small voice asked, "Is that the loving thing to do?" Immediately I said "no" and picked up the towel, putting it in place on the rack.

When I ran out of paper towels one day, I thought,

"Val'll take care of it later." But again the still voice beckoned. And again I realized how selfish that was.

When you multiply such small acts of love by the hundreds of opportunities we can take to help our wives, it adds up. Things like putting your own dishes in the sink or dishwasher after dinner, replacing a light bulb when it burns out, picking up your dirty socks, and putting the clothes into the hamper (instead of *on* it) can lighten her load tremendously. She may not notice. But we are not doing it to be noticed. We are doing it out of love for her and a desire to please the Lord who gives the final reward.

I say this as one who has often been so self-involved that such things are quite a change for me. Maybe for you it is second nature. But that's the place I'm headed. I want such acts of love to become second nature.

These principles of submission have revolutionized my marriage. I share them as one who knows it is a lifetime journey. Just as Tom, the fellow I spoke of at the beginning of this chapter, still has a long way to go as he struggles to submit himself to his wife's needs, I know that it is a battle. But any such marital journey begins with the first act of love.

Still, we come to a question. Some might say, "You've painted a nice picture, Mark, but why is it so hard to act out these principles? Why is submission so tough?"

This calls for dealing with the important issue of how we got into this mess. Planet Earth teems with folks who are rebels, not saints. We would rather be insubordinate than in subjection. Why?

—2— Submission Lost and Regained

That Christmas was special. My first as a Christian. I was excited and exhilarated. Somehow being a new Christian made me think everything in life would work out perfectly from then on. The Lord was wonderful and a wonder worker. No problem was too difficult.

Maybe that was why I disagreed so strongly with my aunt on the subject of marriage. She had said to me, "You have to work at marriage, Mark. It's hard. It takes perseverance, patience, and love."

I was not married at the time. At twenty-two, I dreamed of a day when that lifelong companion would bound into my life. It couldn't be work, I told myself. It would be bliss. Joy. A steady jubilation. When you love one another, things just fit into place. If the Lord is with you, you needn't worry.

Ten years later I married. But only after seeing numerous other marriages break up, even Christian ones. I had to wonder why. Why is it so difficult to make it in marriage? Statistically, over 50% of new marriages do not endure. What is the problem?

The rosy picture I painted in the previous chapter of true biblical submission has gotten out of focus. It has turned into a dismal gray with shades of black. Marriage is nothing close to mutual submission. Too often, it is mutual war. Or, as a little girl who was asked on a Sunday School quiz what Jesus said about people getting married, answered, "Forgive them, for they know not what they do!"

We not only do not know what we did, we still don't know what we are doing. Is this what God intended?

The Original Picture

To understand what God intended submission in marriage to be, we have to go back to the original photograph in Genesis 1 and 2. In those chapters we see the essential ingredients of marriage, what God planned all along.

In God's Image

The first element we notice is that God made man and woman in His image. "And God created man in His own image, in the image of God He created him; male and female He created them" (Genesis 1:27). Some scholars suggest that the image of God was never meant to be complete in Adam alone. He needed his female counterpart to finish the puzzle.

I agree. Because we know that God did everything by His perfect design, the intrinsic differences between men and women intimate that God meant the two together to reflect His likeness. It is the blend that matters. It is a cooperative, team effort.

Be Fruitful and Multiply

Once God established the picture, He gave His first command. "Be fruitful and multiply, and fill the earth" (Genesis 1:28). Again we see the element of mutual submission: cooperation. God intended the two to work together, not one dominating the other or making demands. God made both responsible; both were required to give a part of themselves. To make another being with the reflection of God upon his heart, they had to come together, to unite, to be one.

Subdue the Earth and Rule

But God gave them another command. He told them to subdue the earth and rule over it. The Hebrew words used here are unique. "Subdue" comes from a root that means to "tread down," to "dominate." The idea is that the earth was untamed. It needed someone to turn it into something organized and beautiful. The earth needed hoeing and mowing. The trees needed pruning. Together, the man and woman would cultivate that garden and transform it from something wildly wonderful to something wonderfully usable.

This involved much more than merely making things mesh. It involved naming the animals, studying them, looking after what God had created. God intended that man and woman gain complete mastery and understanding over His creation. They were in charge. They were to bring everything else into submission.

When God said man was to "rule" over creation, He

meant that we were to "chastise or discipline" it. This pictures an earth that is resistant to the touch. Man and woman would struggle against it to bring it into line. To be sure, God had not created it like a writhing monster that had to be beaten down. But He was giving the first marital partners a challenge. "Run this show together and make it work! But I'll be here to keep it from becoming too difficult."

We immediately get a picture of a husband and wife working together in a true partnership to make their world something beautiful. Again, we see the mutual submission, the team mentality.

Not Good to be Alone

When we get to chapter two of Genesis, Moses goes back to the first moments of creation and zeroes in more closely on the creation of man and woman. In the first chapter, he gave us the overall view. Now he's going to zoom in on one part of the picture.

After God created Adam in the garden and told him about the tree of good and evil, God knew that something more had to be done. He said, "It is not good for the man to be alone" (Genesis 2:18).

The word "alone" grasps at that most important element of man's nature: God's image was not complete in the male half only. There needed to be a union of male and female. Man could not remain isolated, cut off, separate, divided from his other half.

One more time we see that amazing submission. God had to put Himself beneath the needs of His creature. He had to act on Adam's behalf. He couldn't be satisfied with anything less than the man's complete fulfillment and happiness. So he made "a helper suitable for him."

The Helper Suitable

When God said He would make Adam a "helper," He was not proposing someone inferior, lower, less able, or weak.

God Himself often refers to Himself as our "helper." Look at Psalm 33:20. "Our soul waits for the Lord; He is our help (or "helper"—same word as in Genesis 2:18) and our shield." "God is our refuge and strength, A very present help in trouble" (Psalm 46:1). "For thou hast been my help, and in the shadow of Thy wings I sing for joy" (Psalm 63:7).

When God said He would make Adam a "helper," He meant someone who would aid and support him where he was weak. One of my professors used to say a helper was "one who filled up the empty spaces." Eve colored in the parts where Adam was blank. Eve would become Adam's perfect counterpart—the completion, the consummation, the crowning touch.

Moreover, she would be someone "suitable" to him. The word relates to a root which means someone who is "conspicuous." Not only would Eve fill up the empty spaces, but she would be a highly visible part of his life. Adam might give a lion a hug, a camel a nice rap on the hump, and the hippo a pat on the snout, but he did not spend his time with them. It was his "helper" who was always there. She participated in every aspect of his life.

Do you see the picture? Together, the man and woman were a blend of many strengths and abilities. Together, they were the image of God. Together, they were to rule the earth. Together, they found fulfillment and joy.

Bone of My Bones

The way God impressed all this on Adam is interesting. He had him name the animals. In the process, Adam had the opportunity to inspect each one to see whether it was "suitable" for him.

Can you visualize the scene? Creature after creature lines up. Adam names them and sends them on their way with a friendly pat. But no helper is found who would complement him. Adam's a bit depressed. He didn't realize how alone he was. Maybe he could make it with . . . Adam runs through the list: the koala bear . . . a chimpanzee . . . a lioness. But he only shakes his head. "I'll never find someone to love."

But God knows just what to do. He puts Adam to sleep, takes a rib, and fashions Eve. When Adam wakes up, she is standing there—and not even across a crowded room. This is his very own enchanted moment. He cries, "This is now bone of my bones and flesh of my flesh!" Adam was saying, "This is what I've been waiting for. This is the one who's like me, but unlike me. This is the one I can spend my life with! This is the one who completes me." Adam could not have taken a day with a bear, an hour with a chicken, or a minute with a cobra. But he saw instantly that he could become one with Eve.

I have to stop here a moment and reflect. Isn't this an incredible portrait? Talk about paradise! What man could ask for more?

I remember turning thirty years old with no woman in sight. And then my wife came along. I spotted her there in church. Something inside of me said, "Wow!"

I thought I was in paradise. Indeed, maybe God gives us a little taste of it in those first crimson flushes of love when little bursts of color explode in our minds as we see her walk down the street. This is what it was meant to be, wasn't it—joy, fulfillment, completion? Do you remember how you felt? Think back and re-savor those feelings.

Leave, Cleave, and Become One Flesh

Nonetheless, the picture is not finished yet. Moses comments in verse 24, "For this cause a man shall leave his father and mother, and shall cleave to his wife; and they shall become one flesh."

This is the climax in technicolor. He shall "leave," break ties with his parents, and establish a new home. He shall "cleave"—the word means to "glue something together." And he shall "become one flesh." This is much more than an act of sexual intercourse. It is a total fusing of two lives into one. This is where the two streams become one river, where the two gears meet and run the machine, where the torn halves of the dollar bill are brought together to make a whole.

Submission Personified

The whole scenario of the marriage of Adam and Eve depicts perfectly what God intended in marriage from the start. It was a mutual cooperation, a perfect commingling, a blending of two whose primary objective and concern was the satisfaction and fulfillment of the other. For in fulfilling his other half, he fulfilled himself. Adam was still the head. He led. But the way he led was to be through submission to the Lord, to truth, to what was right, not what was selfish.

The Picture Shattered

Yet, just as the family portrait is hung on the wall, it is shattered. Satan steps into the garden, tempts Eve, and

Adam follows. The whole building collapses. Suddenly, the two no longer live in mutual submission. Now, selfishness and egoism invade their marriage. Look at what happens.

1. *Respect and openness are banished.* The moment they eat of the fruit, they both see that they are naked. But is it just the physical nakedness they see? No, it is the recognition of one another as sinners, as breakers of the law. They are embarrassed in each another's presence. Suddenly, they know what each has become, and they are ashamed.

This is still true in our world. When the original design of mutual submission collapsed, we inherited the rubble. We can no longer be honest with one another. We refuse to speak the truth. We hide, bob, weave, and dance about. And we never get quite close enough to know one another intimately. In a marriage without submission, there is no possibility of true intimacy. Both partners are too afraid to reveal their true selves. They might be rejected by the other.

2. *Hiding from God.* Where before there was perfect communion, now there is fear. They do not want God to see them, to be with them, to walk with them, to talk with them. They want to run. First, they try to hide from one another. Then they try to hide from God.

Again, this is what happens in marriage. A couple keeps God at arm's length. They don't want Him intruding on their "privacy." They don't want Him and His Word rocking their foundations.

3. *Inability to admit guilt and rectify the situation.* When God designed marriage, He meant it to be a harmonious cooperation. But when God asks Adam what has happened, he immediately blames Eve. "The woman whom Thou gavest to be with me, she gave me from the

tree, and I ate" (Genesis 3:12). When God asks the woman what she did, she blames the serpent.

Suddenly the partners have become like small children, refusing to accept responsibility. Thus, the world's marriages are plagued with revenge, games, manipulation, anger, and hot words. We refuse to deal with the true issue. If one confronts the other about a sin, the other merely denies it and argues that he is not the one to blame.

The Curse

But if these natural consequences to sin did not totally ruin the design, the curse God pronounces on them (and on all marriages forever after) did. Notice several elements of the curse.

First, Eve would undergo multiplied pain in childbirth (Genesis 3:16). Naturally, this could have a tremendous effect not only on the woman's desire to have children, but also to get married. Sexual relations could be accompanied by great fear. The beautiful freedom enjoyed before the sin in the garden would be curbed. A struggle between man and woman would ensue.

Second, Eve would desire to dominate her husband. The prospective pain of childbirth could make the woman reject sexual relations altogether. Some interpret this to mean that God curbed it by adding this one blessing—the wife would still "desire" her husband despite the anticipated pain.

However, it has not worked out that way in reality. Sex is often a battleground for husbands and wives, and men through all the ages have lamented woman's weaker sexual urge. What else could this "desire" be?

This expression occurs only one other place in Scripture, Genesis 4:7, where God tells Cain that sin is trying to overwhelm him. Here, an identical rendering is found (except for the pronouns). Compare the two verses.

Genesis 3:16	Genesis 4:7
"Your desire shall be for your husband, and he shall rule over you."	*"Its [sin] desire is for you, but you must master it."*

God is saying that Eve would desire to dominate her husband, just as sin wanted to overcome Cain. This becomes a part of the curse. Eve will strive to control, manipulate, rule, and run her husband's decisions and desires.

Isn't that precisely what we see in many of the marriages around us? It is part of the curse. Fulfillment in marriage becomes a near impossibility.

But that is not all. The curse goes on to say that Adam would become the first male chauvinist.

When Eve tries to dominate him, what will he do? The biblical expression is, "He shall rule over you" (Genesis 3:16). The word here for "rule" is not the same word we found earlier in Genesis 1:28 where Adam and Eve were told to "rule" over the earth in a benign, kindly sort of rule. No, this "rule" is the kingly, crush-him-down-and-become-an-imperial-master sort of thing. Adam would, in effect, become the typical chauvinist, crushing his wife, fighting against her, and seeking with all his power to make her do only what he wants.

The conclusion of this third point is that the curse has led to the whole war between the sexes. And it has been going on since Adam and Eve left the garden! There is no real cooperation, no genuine submission. Man and woman are locked in a battle. They cannot get away from their loneliness and need for companionship, so they marry. But once in it, all they think about is that they want to get out of it.

Marriages do not have to be like this. And many aren't. Any husband or wife, by godly willpower, can change his way of relating to his spouse so that general goodness and kindness reigns. However, the mutual and perfect submission which God created originally has been lost.

Still, there is a fourth result of the curse: The husband would find it difficult to be fulfilled through work. The earth would produce mostly thorns, thistles, and weeds (Genesis 3:17-19). He would now sweat in the fields and like it very little.

This element would make marriage very difficult also. To produce something worthwhile, he would have to spend most of his day at work. The husband would not function solely as husband anymore. Wife ends up complaining that she never sees him, and he complains that she complains!

Perhaps, at this moment, you are saying, "My marriage isn't like that. I'm really very happy. My wife and I have a beautiful relationship." Many marriages do rise above the power of the curse and make something good of their relationship. The important thing is that marriage was intended for something far greater.

The Solution

What then is the solution? What is that greater something? Are we condemned to live out the results of Adam and Eve's sin? Are we doomed to live with the negative sign the curse placed in front of marriage when God placed His punishment on us for our parents' sin?

Absolutely not. God has broken the power of the curse. How? In Jesus Christ.

When Christ died on the cross, He made it possible for

husbands, wives, and children to be made new, to be born again, to start over without the obliterating effects of the curse dogging them every step. Paul wrote that when we become Christians we are "a new creature; the old things passed away; behold, new things have come" (II Corinthians 5:17). In John 10:10 Jesus tells us that He came that we "might have life, and might have it abundantly." Christ makes us free (Galatians 5:1). As a result, we can reestablish the order and organization God created in the first marriage. Mutual submission is regained! In Christ, our marriages can become what God intended.

Why the Curse?

But that leads to an important question: Why the curse? Wasn't God being a bit harsh?

The curse is actually an act of great grace—because the curse drives people to God. When we struggle and fight within our marriages trying to find fulfillment, trying to terminate selfishness, bitterness, and resentment, we only become more deeply mired in them. We are driven to despair. But that very despair is what often propels people to the Lord. They realize they have nowhere else to go.

The curse is what makes us unable to accept submission. But when we turn to God, we find we can enjoy it together. We are free to turn to Christ and seek His help, power, control, and wisdom.

Only in Christ, by uniting through faith to the Lord of creation, can a man begin to live by the principles outlined in the first chapter. Only in Christ can he truly put his wife's needs first. Only in Christ can he do what is right and enjoy it regardless of the actions of others. Only in Christ can he entrust his own needs to God. And only in Christ can he believe that God will honor him.

In Christ, too, we reclaim the full image of God and can

begin to express His character in our lives. We begin to regard each other as a team again, working together toward similar goals. We strive to be helpers to one another—to leave, cleave, and become one flesh . . . a process, not a one-time event. It's all possible. But only in Christ. He alone has broken the power of sin. He alone accomplishes freedom from guilt. He alone fills us with His Spirit and teaches us each day to walk closer to Him.

That is what gives me hope and joy. That is what assures me that things are working out, getting better, moving forward. Though we sin, we repent, learn, and grow through it. Though we take two steps backward, we are still forging three steps forward. If it wasn't for Jesus, I am sure we would have given up long ago. But with Him anything is possible. Everything is possible.

A Question

Yet, a question arises. If all of this is true, if a husband can be and should be in a state of mutual submission, how does the idea of "headship" fit in? Am I not "head" of my home? Do I not answer to God for the condition and management of my family?

Let's look at what biblical headship is, and how it relates to the idea of submission.

—3—
Biblical Headship and Heartship

A farm boy said to his father one day, "Dad, Mary and I plan to get married. But we can't seem to agree on who's going to be boss. I need some advice."

The father answered, "No doubt about it, this decision will affect yours and Mary's happiness for all your lives. This is what you should do. Get out the wagon, load up a hundred leghorn pullets, and hitch the brown mare and the old black mare to the wagon. Then head off down the road. Stop at each house and ask who the boss is. If the woman says she is, give her a chicken. If the man says he is, give him a mare. When you run out of chickens or mares, you'll have your answer."

The fellow thought this a fine idea, so he went out. By evening he'd visited all the houses but one. He had only one chicken left. He still had both mares.

He approached the last house nervously. After knocking and explaining his problem to the man who answered, he asked who the boss was. The man said, "I am." The boy was startled, considering all that had happened, but he said, "Okay, come on out and pick out your mare." The old man inspected the horses carefully for spavines and lameness and everything else, and even opened their mouths and checked the teeth to see how old they were. Finally he said, "I'll take the brown." All this time the wife had been watching hard-eyed from the porch. In a calm, stern voice she yelled, "Harry, take the black." Harry turned and said, "I'll take the black." Instantly, the lad said, "Mister, you'll take a chicken."

An Old Problem

Who is the boss in the home is an ancient problem. Domineering females and chauvinistic males have lived and died for centuries, and their struggle continues. But for the Christian, the problem would seem to be settled by a few authoritative verses. "The man is the head of a woman" (I Corinthians 11:3). "Wives, be subject to your own husbands, as to the Lord. For the husband is the head of the wife, as Christ also is head of the church" (Ephesians 5:22-23).

The word "be subject" is a military term. A private was subject to a sergeant. A sergeant was subject to a lieutenant.

The word "head" also relates to authority. The same word was used of a capstone or keystone in an arch, of a capital city, and of rank in an organization. The "head" was he with whom the buck stopped. He had the final say, but he also had the final responsibility. Just as people answered to him, so a "head" also answered to those in authority over him.

In Paul's Day

What then is biblical headship? Let's take a brief look at the times in which Paul wrote.

Marriage in Paul's day would strike many with amusement today. William Barclay provides some poignant information in his commentary on Ephesians (pp. 169-170). The Jews regarded women as less than human. Many prayed each morning, "Thank you, Jehovah, for not making me a Gentile, a slave, or a woman." Jewish law did not even recognize women as people. They were "things." They had no legal rights.

Worse than that was the divorce situation. Two schools predominated in Jewish thinking. One was that of Shammai, who interpreted Deuteronomy 24:1 (the primary Old Testament passage on divorce) to mean that divorce was lawful only in the case of adultery on the part of the wife.

The school of Hillel, an equally respected authority, interpreted Moses differently. They said that Moses sanctioned divorce for nearly anything. If a wife burned the lamb, left dust under the bed, or walked in public with her head uncovered, the husband could divorce her. Anything went. Today, Erma Bombeck captured the same idea when she wrote colorfully of a man who was divorcing his wife because she didn't "spread the mayonnaise all the way to the edge of the bread." A Jew could argue seriously for such a thing in Paul's day!

The Greeks were not much better. A wife owed her husband absolute obedience. Men had wives for procreation and to run the affairs of their homes. Few Greeks would ever have thought of a wife as a friend, lover, or comrade-in-passion. She led a life of seclusion and was not even allowed to appear on the streets alone. Her husband could divorce her for any reason, at a word. The only security she had was that if he divorced her, he must return her dowry.

The Romans, however, were the worst. Men married, then cast aside their wives with abandon. Divorce was rampant. Seneca recorded that women dated the years by the names of their husbands. Barclay says that Jerome "declares it to be true that in Rome there was a woman who was married to her twenty-third husband and she herself was his twenty-first wife." Not even Hollywood has outdone that!

A Matter of Function

But actually, this matter of headship is not so difficult. Headship is a matter of role and function. it has nothing to do with superiority, intelligence, ability, or brute force. It does not even mean that the head is always right or has the only opinion in a matter.

In any situation that requires organizing people to accomplish a task, we must delineate function and role. How do I relate to all those workers in the office? How does the secretary? The president? The executive officer? If each does not have a function within the organization, if there is no framework within which we all operate, anarchy reigns. All successful organizations learn to mesh their gears so that it all runs together smoothly.

The human body itself is an incredible example of such headship. The brain tells the legs to walk to the store because the stomach says, "Let's eat." But if the big toe gets stubbed and requires care, the brain decides that the stomach will have to put its needs on hold.

In the home, headship means everyone has a function and role to perform. Organization and order are the priorities.

In the beginning God decided the husband would be

the "head." He helps everyone else to blend their skills together.

How husbands do this, though, varies greatly. Some act like Army sergeants, snapping orders, demanding instant obedience. Other husbands act like kings. Everyone is there to serve him. Still others lay around and do nothing. Mom (or someone else), in frustration, beings leading because nothing would get done otherwise.

Who is right?

The Preeminent Head

Amazingly, God offers husbands much freedom in working out their headship. The place to get a clear picture of "headship" in marriage, though, is not in any individual marriage. Rather, it is in the head of the church, Jesus Christ. The church is His bride, soon to be His wife. If we want to see how a "head" conducts himself, look at Him.

How, then, does Jesus express His headship?

What follows is a close look at a number of characteristics of Jesus' expression of headship in the New Testament. This is not an exhaustive analysis. But it is a start.

Submission and Obedience to the Father

The first element of Jesus' headship might startle many. It is found in I Corinthians 11:3: "Christ is the head of every man, and the man is the head of a woman, and God is the head of Christ."

"God is the *head* of Christ?" Wait a second! Aren't the Father and Jesus two distinct members of the Trinity? Aren't they equal?

Yes. But headship has nothing to do with equality or superiority. It has everything to do with function. Even though Jesus Christ is fully God, equal to the Father in power, wisdom, knowledge, holiness, and divinity, He still has a role to perform.

That is an important point. Jesus Himself is "under authority." In fact, He submitted so completely that He became "obedient to the point of death, even death on a cross" (Philippians 2:8). Even though He longed to avoid the cross, in the same breath He said, "Yet not as I will, but as Thou wilt" (Matthew 26:39).

This is the way God has organized creation. He has invested it with order, efficiency, law, beauty, and excellence by causing all things to relate to one another with differing degrees of authority and power—even Jesus to the Father and the Spirit to the Son.

In this regard, the primary element of a husband's headship is that he be in submission to Jesus Christ. "Christ is the head of every man" (I Corinthians 11:3). He manifests his submission by knowing, following, and obeying Jesus.

This struck me once when I overheard a seminary couple arguing in the apartment next to mine. "You're not in submission to me!" shouted the husband. "But you're not in submission to Jesus!" cried the wife. They hacked and sawed away at one another. But sooner or later one had to decide to do what was right regardless of the mate's actions. I like to think that the husband woke up first. Wives have little trouble submitting to husbands who are tuned in to Jesus. It is those who clench their fists and demand submission who never get it.

Responsibility

The second element of headship is responsibility and accountability.

Jesus Christ holds every husband accountable for the way his family is managed. Jesus will never ask the wife how well she did running the household. If the home goes bankrupt, He will never say to the wife, "Why didn't you take better care of your money?" If the kids end up in jail, He will not question the wife by saying, "What happened, lady?" Headship means Dad is responsible. He answers to his Head for how things turn out.

One day at work, my boss informed me that our plant would have an inspection. "Get it spiffed up perfect. All the dignitaries are coming, and they need to see something remarkable."

I countered, "But there's only one worker down at the plant. And he's overworked as it is. I don't know whether he can do it."

"He?" he asked.

I looked him in the eye. "Uh, I don't know what you mean."

He said, "I don't care what *he* does. I'm concerned about what *your* plant looks like. You're responsible for it. Whatever you have to do to get it in shape, do it. But I hold you accountable."

I began to sweat just a little bit.

But how many times do I try to swing the blame onto my wife when things go wrong in the family? That doesn't work with Jesus Christ. He wants to know, "How did *you* lead? How did *you* manage the home? How did things go under *your* direction?"

That puts a new twist on the whole headship issue. Most of us think of headship as a great thing. "I get to tell everyone what to do." "Whatever I say goes!" Sure, a head has authority. But with such authority goes responsibility. The head of every home answers to the head of every man—Jesus Christ!

Authority

And that brings us to a third element of headship we see in Jesus—authority. In order for a leader to get people to do what he says, he must have authority.

Now authority is a strange thing. In one sense it comes from above. When a policeman comes up behind us with siren blowing and lights flashing, we pull over. Why? Because the state has given him authority. We obey that man regardless of the kind of person he is. He can be the worst of the worst, but that car and uniform have power.

On the other hand, true authority has something more. When Jesus preached the Sermon on the Mount, Matthew writes that "the multitudes were amazed at His teaching; for He was teaching them as one having authority, and not as their scribes" (Matthew 7:28-29).

Clearly, Jesus did not wear a uniform that said, "If you don't listen to Me, the Father will get you!" What He had was intrinsic to His person. He spoke with a seriousness and air of authority that made people stop and listen. Even more than that, when He taught, He did not equivocate. When the scribes taught, they would say, "Well, Hillel says this about this passage, and Shammai says this, and I think it means this, but on the other hand, there's Rabbi Akiba who says . . . . " People often came away confused, and probably frustrated.

But Jesus expressed His truths with authority. "You have heard that it was said . . . but *I* say to you . . . . "

Yet, it was not bombast or personal confidence that clanged with authority. It was that the truth He spoke was convincing. It rang true. It made sense. People found their hearts in agreement.

Moreover, they had seen His miracles. They had witnessed His character. His authority not only came from above, but also from the kind of person He was! He had the dignity, self-assurance, unswerving conviction, and flawless character that made people respect Him.

True headship involves not only *given* authority—the fact that God says the husband is the head of his home—but *earned* authority—because of the kind of life and character a father displays before his family.

Unconditional Love

A fourth element of true headship is *agape* or unconditional love. Paul wrote, "Husbands love your wives just as Christ also loved the church" (Ephesians 5:25). How did Christ love the church? Unconditionally. He did not say, "I'll love you if you obey me." Or, "I love you because you're so cute." No, it was unconditional. "I love you regardless of anything you are and do."

What is unconditional love? Paul reveals a number of elements.

1. *Sacrifice.* Unconditional love calls for "sacrifice." Jesus "gave Himself up" for the church (Ephesians 5:25). A husband who spends his life on his own whims and uses his family for his own ends may be the physical head of his home, but he won't be the spiritual head. His family's heart simply will not be with him. It is like the story of the small boy, disciplined by his father and told to sit down at dinner. The son protests, "Dad, I may be sitting down on the outside, but I'm standing up on the inside!"

Sacrifice, however, wins a family's heart and soul. And headship becomes a reality because the family submits out of love and respect, not fear.

2. *Servanthood.* Unconditional love means a servant spirit. When Paul said the husband should "give himself up" for his wife, he pictured not only sacrifice, but servanthood. Jesus told His disciples, "You know that the

rulers of the Gentiles lord it over them, and their great men exercise authority over them. It is not so among you, but whoever wishes to become great among you shall be your servant, and whoever wishes to be first among you shall be your slave; just as the Son of Man did not come to be served, but to serve, and to give His life a ransom for many" (Matthew 20:25-28).

It must have been an amazing scene for the disciples to watch as Jesus took off His cloak in the upper room, tied a towel about His waist, and knelt down to wash their feet (John 13). Even more astonishing to them was the way He paid attention to the widows, children, lepers. He always had time to give a little more.

A husband who wants to offer his family unconditional love, and thereby exercise true headship, will be a servant.

This often hits me in little ways. One evening I was sitting in our recreation room watching television. Suddenly, it occurred to me that my wife, who was attending an aerobics class, would be coming home in the dark. "You ought to turn on the outside light," a little voice inside me said. "Ahhhh, she can find the door," another voice answered. A third voice cried, "Yeah, and why should you have to miss part of your show for her?" Instantly I was on my feet. "This is my wife we're talking about!" I went upstairs and flipped the switch.

On another occasion we were listening to some music, and it struck me how nice a bowl of popcorn would be. But should I suggest it? What if Val said, "Yes, why don't *you* make some?" I sat there hoping for a bolt of inspiration to strike her. Then it occurred to me, "Why *don't* you make the popcorn?" I decided to take the plunge.

Those are two little things. But there are multitudes of

them every day, every week. It is the accumulation of little acts of service that show the servant's heart.

3. *Sanctification.* Another element of unconditional love is the desire to bring holiness and purity into family life. Jesus gave Himself up for the church "that He might sanctify her" (Ephesians 5:26). Real love always seeks and honors such qualities as chastity, purity, honesty, integrity, goodness.

To "sanctify" means to "separate for special use." In this passage, it refers to Christ's work in separating us to the Father for His wholehearted and exclusive service as well as bringing us out of the world and away from the influence of Satan. Jesus did not just want a submissive disciple; He wanted a holy, godly one.

Even so, a husband wielding true spiritual headship will develop his wife, lead her spiritually, and desire to see her grow in holiness.

4. *Selflessness.* In the same passage, Paul says that husbands "ought also to love their own wives as their own bodies. He who loves His own wife loves himself" (Ephesians 5:28).

Jesus sees the church as His own body, an extension of Himself. He is not just Himself; He is more. The church is spiritually connected to Him just as the arms are connected to the trunk of a human body.

Selflessness is one of those characteristics we praise, but few make any effort to live. It is incredibly hard. When I think of the multitude of ways I am selfish in my home, I cringe. It is so easy to clatter up the sidewalk, walk in the door, kiss the wife, rumple the three-year-old's hair, and crumple onto the sofa. "Don't bother me now for an hour." Then Val calls from the kitchen. "Mark, the trash is overflowing into the dining room. Will you take it out, or should I wait 'til it overflows into the living room?" That wakes me up. Why should she have to ask me more than once to do something I should do anyway?

On Sundays I usually dress our daughter to give Val more time to get ready for church. But it wasn't always that way. There came a point when I had to decide, "Will you begin truly helping out around here, or does some disaster have to happen to wake you up?"

Selflessness is when you anticipate the trash situation and take it out before your wife says a word. Selflessness is seeing the toddler looking at the book and offering to read it before she patters over. Selflessness is offering to help with the dishes even when you would rather read.

That is hard. But that is what a head does. He sees the needs of his body—his wife as well as himself—and meets them.

5. *Sustenance.* A fifth element of unconditional love is sustenance, the willingness to provide for the care and feeding (physically, emotionally, and spiritually) of the wife. Paul says that a husband who loves his wife as much as himself "nourishes and cherishes (her), just as Christ also does the church" (Ephesians 5:29). If you love someone, you meet their needs as if they were your own.

For instance, when your stomach growls and you glance at your watch, you don't have an argument with your body as to whether you are hungry and deserve something to eat, do you? No, you go get something to eat. When you cut a finger, you don't tell the finger you are too busy reading the paper to patch up the problem, do you? No, you go bandage it.

Similarly, a true head will see his family's needs and meet them. This is as simple as working to provide money for the needs of the home, and as complex as taking her to Chateau Pierre for your anniversary. It is as plain as showing some sympathy about a nasty remark someone made to her that day in the supermarket, and as painful as using the $75.00 you'd been saving for a fishing trip to get her the tennis racket she's been wanting.

6. *Solidity.* The last element of unconditional love is that it is permanent, solid, lasting. "For this cause a man shall leave his father and mother, and shall cleave to his wife" (Ephesians 5:31). That clcaving is as strong as Supcr Glue, as enduring as granite. It simply does not break.

Husbands foster tremendous insecurity in the home when they make threats or suggestions that divorce is an option. A friend told me how arguments with his wife escalate. She'd say something like, "Well, maybe I should move out." He responds, "Okay, so you're going to leave? Then leave, and quit threatening it! I don't care!" And, "Since we can't seem to work this out, maybe a much more permanent solution is necessary." Then he told me he could not understand why his wife was so insecure!

No true head resorts to such tactics. A true husband vows loyalty at the altar and then delivers. I have found that you have to work at refusing to make threats when you are angry. It is a discipline. But that is the very nature of love, isn't it? What kind of love abuses her when she doesn't agree? What kind of head deserts his home when things get tough? A true head is true through thick, thin, and everything else.

Leadership

Still, there is one more element of true headship: leadership. A head is above all a leader. The great French writer Moliere was asked why, in some countries, the king could take the crown at age fourteen, but could not marry until age eighteen. He answered, "Because it is more difficult to rule a wife than a kingdom."

Leadership is probably the hardest part of true headship, yet it is the one element most husbands think they can perform without a thought. Once he wades in, though, he finds that this is one of the most troubling elements of marriage. "She just won't listen to me." "She thinks I'm an idiot." "She won't follow my lead." "She always has a better way." "If I don't give in to her, it's all over for the rest of the week."

So how do you get a free-spirited, strong-willed, sure-minded, determined young lady to follow your lead?

Jesus exemplifies all that is best in leadership. We can see this in the way He led the disciples. Let's look at several elements of His leadership style which are applicable in the headship issue.

He took the initiative. Jesus invited men to follow Him. He sought them out. He did not wait for them to "wake up and smell the coffee." He went where they were, invited them as they were, and took them where He was going. A husband initiates. He does not wait for his wife to start something; he jumps in himself.

He set the example. Repeatedly we see Jesus leading by example. He cast out demons, then gave the disciples authority to do so. He preached the message, then sent them out. He touched lepers, then instructed the disciples to heal. He reached out to little children. He took off His coat and washed the disciples' feet. Similarly, the head of the home leads by blazing the trail with gentle footprints, not by blazing away with verbal bullets.

He delegated authority. Jesus did not crowd anyone out. He shared His gifts. He encouraged one with an ability and sent him out to use it. He gave the disciples tremendous authority to lay the foundation of the church. Headship does not mean we overwhelm our wives or club them into submission. She's a *help*mate, and we listen to her counsel, consider her opinion, give her authority in those areas for which she is best suited.

He developed His followers. Jesus' first invitation contained an awesome promise: "Follow Me, and I will make you become fishers of men" (Mark 1:17). He planned to make something of them. Thus, a leader develops his wife as a spiritual person. He opens up the petals of the flower of her heart, her mind, her soul.

He gave His followers undivided attention when they had a need. When Nicodemus crept out of the night into Jesus' life, Jesus listened. He gave Nicodemus His complete attention. As Jesus stood by the wall and talked with the sinful woman of Sychar, He did not get His drink and then ignore her. Even so, a true head offers his wife a listening ear when she needs it. He does not glance over the edge of the newspaper with a crinkled brow of exasperation when she wants to talk.

He communicated total acceptance. It always amazes me how easy it is to miss the little flourishes in Scripture. Such a one is Jesus' consistent manner in healing lepers. He touched them. Why? To communicate love, acceptance. Lepers had been rejected by everyone. A leader shows his family how much he loves it. He communicates acceptance by restraining his criticism and pouring out his compliments and encouragements.

He had a passion and enthusiasm for His bride. One verse that has always thrilled me is Zephaniah 3:17: "The Lord your God is in your midst, a victorious warrior. He will exult over you with joy, He will be quiet in His love, He will rejoice over you with shouts of joy." Such is His enthusiasm for His own. So also a leader exults for joy and hugs his wife frequently!

He was loyal. I like the scene in Luke 10:38-42 where Martha complains about Mary sitting at Jesus' feet while

Martha fixed dinner. Jesus was loyal to Mary without putting Martha down. He said, "Martha, Martha, you are worried and bothered about so many things; but only a few things are necessary, really only one, for Mary has chosen the good part, which shall not be taken away from her." A real leader supports his followers no matter how many mistakes they make.

We could draw out many other qualities and illustrations of Jesus' conduct as a leader, but these are all elements that should find their way into a leadership style. This is true biblical headship. A husband does not suppress his wife. He does not pretend he is better than she. He does not refuse to hear her part. Rather, he is the leader—in example, in word, in thought. He may not always be right. But he submits to the Lord Jesus, accepts responsibility for the management of his home, expresses unconditional love, and leads in godly authority.

As I look over these words, I find myself reeling. "Good grief! I'm not able to do all this! I'll never cut it!" But I am not in it alone. As I submit myself to Christ's headship, He promises to draw out of me His best, my best. He will do the same for any husband who submits before Him and says, "You are Lord. Make me what I ought to be."

Yet, there is much more. What qualities should characterize a husband who seeks to be the head of his home and in submission to Christ? In the next chapter we will take a look at the characteristics of a submissive man.

—4—

Portrait of a Man in Submission to Christ

Great portraits often bother me. When I visit the National Gallery of Art in Washington or some other famous art museum, I am sometimes shocked at the way artists chose to paint their benefactors. Some of those stern faces and homely countenances could stop a grizzly in his tracks. I often wonder what kind of wife or husband the person was. Some look like the type who wouldn't let you get away with anything. Others are so rigid, you wonder if the fellow was alive or dead at the time of the painting.

But if a wife painted her husband's portrait, what would she put down on the canvas? Face red with fury, his mouth open wide with a strong expression? Or perhaps a tucked chin, drawn brows, and a pointing finger? Or maybe just a newspaper held up high so no one can see over or through it.

One fiancée selected what she thought was an excellent Christmas gift for her husband-to-be, a book called *A Perfect Gentleman.* A year later, after their vows were said and she had had more exposure, she decided on another book gift: *Wild Animals I Have Known.*

What portrait would *your* wife paint? In other words, what kind of character do you demonstrate in your home?

Character is critical. How a husband acts in his home is how he is in reality. Like Dr. Howard Hendricks says, "If your Christianity doesn't work in your home, it doesn't work. Don't export it!"

For that reason, we need to examine what a submissive man is. What characteristics distinguish him from the run-of-the-mill and the rest-of-the-heap?

There are many passages of Scripture we could go to in seeking a portrait of the truly submissive man—the man subject to Christ. An excellent passage is Galatians 5:22-23, the list of the fruit of the Spirit. "But the fruit of the Spirit is love, joy, peace, patience, kindness, goodness, faithfulness, gentleness, self-control." These nine elements of the Spirit's fruit are a direct result of true submission to Christ. "But I say, walk by the Spirit, and you will not carry out the desire of the flesh" (Galatians 5:16). Submission to Christ comes through reliance on the Spirit. Let's examine these character traits.

Love

The first fruit Paul emphasizes is love. The word is *agape*. We looked at this word in the previous chapter under the title "unconditional love." *Agape* is, by its definition, unconditional. It keeps on loving regardless of circumstances, conditions, or response.

The most basic element of such love is not emotion or thought, it is action. *Agape* acts. It does what is right and best for someone. And it does it regardless of how the loved one responds.

One way in which I am experiencing this in my marriage is through asking myself, "Is this the loving thing to do?" When I am about to make a retort to Valerie, I find that still small voice querying, "Is this the *loving* way to deal with this situation?" After I take my shower in the morning and notice the soap lying in a puddle on the floor, it occurs to me, "How would love act? Leave the soap there, or pick it up so Val doesn't have to clean herself with mush?" In fact, I even began praying that the Lord would remind me of all the ways I can begin loving my wife. It has created an amazing transformation in my mind, heart, and actions.

As simple as it may seem, love in the home comes down to little more than asking the question, "Is this the way I would want to be treated?" It is the Golden Rule—"Do unto your wife as you would have her do unto you."

Ask yourself how you like to be treated (Matthew 7:12). I recently thought through some of the things I like—even expect—in a relationship:

1. I like to be listened to when I have a gripe.
2. I like a straightforward answer, not an evasive dodge.
3. I like to be forgiven when I request it and not have it brought up again at a later date.
4. I like to have my money promptly.
5. I like to be given the benefit of the doubt.
6. I like it when my requests are given the same attention that others get.

Now transpose those "likes" to your wife. When we treat her the way we would like to be treated, *even when or if she may not treat us that way,* that is when we begin to love in the power of the Spirit.

Joy

Joy is an indispensable part of the husband-wife relationship. Yet, it can evaporate very quickly after the honeymoon. I asked one friend how his home life was. He said, "I've been angry every day for six years!" That is a far cry from the joy Scripture reveals.

Biblical joy is a response to good news. When the wise men saw the star, they "rejoiced exceedingly with great joy" (Matthew 2:10). When the angels appeared to the shepherds to announce Christ's birth, they brought "good news of a great joy" (Luke 2:10).

A man who bears the fruit of joy in his life lives above his bad news. Why? Not because that bad news does not affect him, but because he hears higher and better news. He displays joy because of all that God promises in the Word. When things go wrong, he knows God causes all things to work together for good (Romans 8:28) . . . that he might be conformed more closely to the image of Christ (Romans 8:29). When his wife does not respond to a special effort, he remains confident and joyous that, "He who began a good work in you will perfect it until the day of Christ Jesus" (Philippians 1:6). Joy is a response to truth.

For this reason a submissive man tends toward affability rather than irritability, kindliness rather than whininess, and genuine smiles rather than reluctant grins. It is a matter of walking in the Spirit. When the heart is clean, the outlook is joy. When the heart is filled with ugliness, the outlook is just as murky and dirty.

When I choose to submit to the Holy Spirit, joy not only returns to me, it also revives me. One of my little weekly "chores" is watching our daughter on Saturdays so Valerie can have a chance to shop. One Saturday I arranged myself on the sofa, propped a book before my face, and hoped Nicole would do the same—somewhere else. But she said, "Daddy, can I have a peanut butter sandwich?" I got up, prepared the sandwich, then walked back to the couch. Seconds after settling in, a little voice called from the kitchen, "Daddy, could you put it on a plate for me?" I got up and produced the plate. Went back to the couch. Instants later, the little voice called again, "Daddy, would you cut it up for me?" 'I'll not only cut *it* up,' I thought. But I went in and, with a smile, chopped up the sandwich. I figured, 'What more can there be?' and settled back down. Moments later: "Daddy, can I have a fork?" My temperature was rising, but I got up, tore out a fork and placed it next to her plate. She smiled up at me and said, "Thank you, Daddy." I *knew* there couldn't be anything else.

But sure enough, a split second after I found my niche on the sofa, she said, "Daddy, could I have some milk?" I stomped in. She pointed. "In *that* cup, please!" Absolutely! I went back to my place. Silence. Oh, what lovely silence.

Then, Nicole jumped down and walked into the family room and said, "Daddy, do you love me?" Where do children get these things? And for a moment, I had to think about that one. But then I laughed, hopped up, took her in my arms, and said, "Of course, I love you." She said, "I'm glad," and ran off to get a book for me to read to her. I silently gave thanks anyway.

And my joy returned! Joy is possible when we give

thanks to the God who superintends all circumstances for our good . . . to conform us to the image of His Son.

Peace

Kenneth Mosley wrote, "Every man needs a wife, because sooner or later something goes wrong that you just can't blame on government" (*Reader's Digest,* Sept. 1979). One of the male gender's most difficult problems is his inability to admit when he is wrong. He will pass the buck, grow antlers, and gore the doe before he'll say, "I was wrong; I'm sorry." But that is one of the most important elements of the fruit of peace—repentance.

The spiritual fruit of peace results in more than just a restful countenance. It takes root only in husbands who are no longer at war—with themselves, their wives, and/or God. No longer looking for revenge or a way to get back, he forgives. And when he is wrong, he repents and admits it.

One of the biggest traps a husband can make is to get into the pattern of apologizing to his wife just to get her off his back. The situation is typical. The wife mopes about. Hubby says, "What's wrong?"

She replies, "Oh, nothing." A long sigh.

He grits his teeth. "Okay, what did I do now?"

"Nothing."

They go back and forth until she tells him he ought to know what he did. A fiery splotch of red careens through his mind at this point accompanied by thoughts like, *What am I supposed to do? Read your mind?* But somehow he works up the patience to ask through tightening lips, "Please tell me what I did wrong."

After more minutes of questioning and wrangling, she tells him. To him it seems so insignificant that not even a gnat would choke on it. *Oh, good grief,* he thinks, *this is absurd. I suppose I have to apologize for that?* He grits his teeth. "I'm sorry. Will you forgive me?"

She nods her head.

Then he thinks, *Now, finally, we can move on from it.*

But he has not really changed or repented, has he? And the problem will go on to the next and the next episode. What he is not dealing with is his tendency to be insensitive. A godly man, living in the Spirit's power, will realize that he needs to promote real peace in his home, not this pseudo, seething, embittered, "I'll-apologize-just-to-get-her-off-my-back" attitude.

Patience

The Greek word used here is *makrothumia.* Literally, long-suffering. It occurs most often in situations involving people, not things or circumstances. A husband walking in submission to the Spirit "suffers long."

I suspect that patience, or the lack thereof, comes out in the face of a wife's differences—those traits you wish you could change. I remember reading about a wife whose husband retired. One morning she watched in quiet astonishment as he rearranged all the contents of her kitchen shelves. "Didn't you try to stop him?" a friend asked. "Did you say something to him?"

"No," said the patient wife. "I just waited till he was through. Then I went down to the basement and rearranged his tools" (*Reader's Digest,* July 1980).

That may be laughable, but it is not long-suffering.

When it comes to expressing patience with a mate's foibles, idiosyncrasies and weaknesses, I've discovered three primary and biblical ways patience rears its kindly head.

First, by *acceptance.* Some things cannot be changed. Never. Under any circumstances. The Lord has decreed, "This is the way she is; accept it." They are the marks of her personality or her body that make her who and what she is. Be thankful for them. Without them, she wouldn't be the woman you love.

Charlie Shedd writes in his book, *Letters to Philip,* that women "will do anything in the world for you if you put them at ease about their faults; build up their strong points; and reach that high level of kindness which seems to say, 'The blend is what I like. I love you for what you are *in toto*.' "

Second, by *speaking the truth in love.* Husbands and wives are not to hide their feelings from one another, but to express the truth honestly and forthrightly. How else can we grow? Chapter eight will discuss this in more detail.

Third, by *working together on the problem.* A husband does not "grin and bear it." He comes alongside and seeks to work *with* his wife. "We're in this together, honey, and I'm not giving up on you; so don't you give up on me."

I sometimes think of myself as my wife's coach. And she's my coach. We want to develop one another totally. That takes patience, acceptance, and work. But it is worth it. Our marriage keeps getting better and better.

Kindness

Someone once told me, "Be kind; everyone you meet is fighting a hard battle." That goes for husbands and wives, too. Yet, often the home features less kindness than any other place on earth.

I watched the TV movie, "Murder by Insanity," with

grief and horror. An insane nuclear physicist abuses his wife, then ends up divorced and in an asylum. But he convinces the authorities he is sane. They give him a free pass one day. He buys a hunting knife, and heads for his former wife's house. He breaks in and murders her. The next morning he calls the police to inform them he has finally done what he said he was going to do all along.

Such stories horrify us. But what is more terrifying is that this is no longer just television fiction. Studies reveal that domestic violence is increasing at a ten-alarm-fire rate. Even Christians are not immune. As a pastor, I frequently counseled with people committed to Christ who also committed violence to one another regularly. One wife reached such terror levels that she called me at 1:00 a.m. and asked me to pick her up miles from home. I found her cowering in a slum dwelling, hiding from her husband who had brought her into the porn district on a supposed date.

But kindness is much more than simply being decent to one another. Alain, a French philosopher, wrote, "It is a small thing to accept people for what they are; if we really love them we must want them to be what they are." That's the essence of kindness, the ability to let a person be what he is without picking up a chisel and starting to chop.

I enjoy the *Peanuts* comic strip. One of my favorites features Lucy and Charlie Brown. Lucy cries to Charlie, "Merry Christmas, Charlie Brown." She adds, "At this time of year I think we should put aside all our differences, and try to be kind." Charlie answers, "Why does it have to be for just this time of year? Why can't it be all year around?" Lucy replies, "What are you, some kind of fanatic or something?"

Maybe we should be "that kind of fanatic!"

Kindness is made up of many little acts in the home. The Greek word means generosity, magnanimity of spirit. To be pleasant, easy. A kind person makes things pleasant and smooth. He is not always "pressing his wife to the wall." He is thinking, "What nice thing can I do *now*?" Would it be offering to make some hot chocolate? Or sitting on the couch rubbing her back? Or holding the car door open for her, waiting until she gets in, and then shutting it?

Even when the kindness is overlooked or unnoticed, the kind one does not give up. He presses on with greater acts of kindness. His reward (indeed his goal) is not to be noticed, but to give.

Goodness

The sixth fruit of the Spirit is "goodness." The word is similar to that used for kindness, and it means doing those things that are beneficial, useful. A "good" man does what is right, regardless of what others say or do.

Goodness makes a husband strive to be generous to his wife and lavish in his praise, gifts, deeds, and friendship.

One day my wife came to me and asked for some extra money over her monthly household needs. After an argument, I grudgingly handed her the money. She shook her head and informed me that it made her angry the way I would give money to the church, but with her it required begging. I was cut to the heart. Suddenly it occurred to me that I was not only cheating her of her needs, but myself of joy. I decided then and there to give with a smile, and to my wife above all.

This revolutionizes one's whole outlook toward money and his wife. He begins doing deeds of goodness and kindness because he wants to, not because he must.

Faithfulness

Someone wrote, "Dear Abby," "What factor do you think is the most essential if a woman is to have a lasting marriage?" Abby replied, "A lasting husband" (*Reader's Digest,* Oct. 1981).

To be faithful means to be reliable, loyal. The Greek word carries the idea of true piety, genuine religion, being sincere. It is much more than mere marital fidelity, although that is essential. Charlie Shedd tells his son in *Letters to Philip* that a wife will only love her husband more when she knows he is utterly dependable. "You should look her squarely in the eye and solemnly swear: 'Neither by day or by night will I ever cut you down in company. Not before my family, your family, our family. Not before friends, acquaintances, strangers. When you are with me or behind your back. *Never* by wisecrack, or snide remark, or in any manner do I intend to be anything other than one hundred percent loyal!' "

Can your wife depend on you? To show up when you say you will? To stand by her when she is attacked? To hold your tongue when she makes a mistake before others? To guard your heart in the presence of other women? To meet her needs without argument or grudge?

Perhaps one of marriage's greatest moments of loyalty came when the Titanic went down in 1912. Mr. and Mrs. Isadore Strauss stood together during the loading of the lifeboats, filled only with women and children. They both helped many to climb aboard. Finally, Mr. Strauss, who had urged his wife repeatedly to enter one of the boats, forced her to go. But the moment she was seated, she sprang up and hopped back on deck before her husband could stop her. She caught his arm and snuggled up against him, exclaiming, "We have been long together through a great many years. We are old now. Where you go, I will go."

Gentleness

This often misunderstood fruit is sometimes translated "meekness." It doesn't have anything to do with spiritlessness, weakness, or wimpiness. The word means "power under control." It was used of a horse, broken and tamed, but ready to gallop like the wind at a flick of the bridle.

I once asked a woman what was the one quality women always looked for in men. She said, "Gentleness."

It is a quality husbands often lack. Maybe it is the competitive instinct or the wear of life or the pressure of the workplace that causes us to kick, bite, snarl, and fight. Whatever, the quality of gentleness is not common or easily attained.

Yet, it is not beyond the grasp of anyone. *Time* magazine (1-17-83) mentioned that Wilt Chamberlain, the great basketball star who stood over seven feet tall, possessed both incredible strength and resolute gentleness. In 1,218 professional career games, Wilt the Stilt never once fouled out. Considering the physical nature of the modern basketball game and the passions that can sizzle into flame, that is a remarkable achievement. And a remarkable gentleness.

Someone gave this advice for a happy marriage: "Never yell at each other unless the house is on fire." It is a hard lesson to learn, a difficult trait to nurture.

Self-Control

The last fruit mentioned in Paul's list holds everything else together. The word means "self-mastery," the ability to hold the body, mind, and emotions in complete subjection to the will. Paul pictured it best in I Corinthians 9:25, referring to an athlete: "And everyone who competes in the games exercises self-control in all things."

Self-control, though, is much more than a holding pattern—keeping everything in check even though you would like to explode. That is part of it, yes. But real self-mastery is more than putting a lid on a boiling pot. It is keeping the temperature in the pot just right so that you rarely have to put the lid on it!

You

How do you measure up?

If you answer, "Not so well," don't despair. What matters is that you are seeing these qualities increasing, growing, developing.

The question is: Do you?

SECTION TWO: Commands to Live By

—5—
Live with Your Wife in an Understanding Way

A fellow employee approached me one day with a problem. He said, "My wife is really upset with me, and I can't figure it out. The other night we were talking about a trip I had to take. She was unhappy about it, but I just said it wouldn't be long, and anyway it would be good for my career. We got to talking about careers and such, and suddenly she said, 'I suppose you could get along pretty well without me nowadays, couldn't you?' "

He paused, and his face was a picture of despair. I asked, "So what did you say?"

"That's just it. I thought I gave a pretty good answer. I said, 'Well, in some ways I could get along and in other ways I couldn't. It's not a cut and dry issue.' Then I gave her my thoughts on the advantages and disadvantages of marriage from a man's point of view."

He sighed and added, "That's when things went haywire. Man, I told her all sorts of advantages to marriage! And that the advantages outweighed the disadvantages! But she was so mad, she was ready to strangle me. I can't figure it out."

I had to laugh. I guess I have been there a hundred times. The problem was that my friend's wife was not interested in a logical analysis of the plusses and minuses of marriage. I told him, "What she wanted was some assurance. She wanted you to say you couldn't live without her and would never want to. She wanted you to confirm to her that you still loved her more than ever!"

Suddenly, he exploded, "Well, why didn't she say so?"

"Because she's a woman!"

Suddenly, he grinned and said, "I guess I blew it pretty bad, huh?"

I had to laugh again, but added, "Hang in there long enough, and you'll blow it a million more times!"

Reflecting back on that little discussion, I realized again how far afield we husbands can get in carrying on a healthy, loving relationship with our wives. We tend to be bluntly logical, precise, and factual, but our wives are not always looking for such things. Sometimes all they want is some cuddling, a few kind words, and a listening ear. Or, they'll ask a leading question in order to get to something much deeper.

A husband in submission to his Lord will study this issue. He will want to know everything he can about his wife. He'll make understanding her his number one priority and lifelong ambition. In fact, it will take that long! That is one of the great joys of marriage. You are always finding new and greater traits in your mate—things you never imagined existed.

It all comes together in I Peter 3:7: "You husbands likewise, live with your wives in an understanding way, as with a weaker vessel, since she is a woman . . . " Peter's thought here strikes fire. He literally says, "Dwell with your wives in knowledge . . . . "

The word Peter used for "knowledge" is the same word found in II Peter 1:5 where he said, " . . . in your faith supply moral excellence, and in your moral excellence, knowledge . . . . " What Peter sought to convey was that this kind of knowledge comes from the Holy Spirit. It is experiential heart knowledge, born out of loving observation of our wives. It is knowledge that comes only through intimacy and spiritual discernment.

But some of us never learn to live with our wives in light of that knowledge. We stumble along making mistake after mistake and never really discover that lovely lady who thinks so differently from ourselves.

How then are we to live with our wives in knowlege?

Know Her as a Woman

In my marriage I have discovered three simple elements to Peter's command. The first is that we are to know and understand our wives *as women.* The expression Peter uses is, "Live with her . . . as with a weaker vessel, since she is a woman (3:7)." When he said "weaker vessel," he wasn't referring to intelligence, wisdom, ability, or talents. He meant that she isn't constructed the same way a man is. In fact, a better translation might be, "as with a weaker vessel, since she is *feminine.*"

God made woman "feminine." She was not a rough and tumble counterpart to the man. She was not a helpmate like a middle linebacker is a helper to the left tackle. Rather, she was his "complement," his reverse image. She filled up the empty spots. Where he was weak, she was strong. And vice-versa.

What astonishes me almost daily are the built-in differences between men and women. Before I got married, I thought that women were basically the same as men, except packaged differently. But after some years of marriage, I have to admit I am still constantly amazed at the differences—physically, mentally, emotionally, and spiritually. Women do not think, reason, react, feel, or choose like men. They often have different priorities, values, convictions, hopes, and fears, and it is all because of the way God made them. They are helpmates, soulmates, and first mates, but also mates of a different feather. They are as different as a fork is from a spoon, even though they go together perfectly. Thus, when you get a man and a woman in a lifelong commitment to love, honor, and support one another, there are bound to be differences.

Dr. James Dobson points this out in his book, *What Wives Wish Their Husbands Knew About Women.*

> *An effort has been underway for the past few years to prove that men and women are identical, except for the ability to bear children. Radical feminists have vigorously (and foolishly) asserted that the only distinction between the sexes is culturally and environmentally produced. Nothing could be farther from the truth; males and females differ biochemically, anatomically, and emotionally. In truth, they are unique in every cell of their bodies, for men carry a different chromosomal pattern than women. There is also considerable evidence to indicate that the hypothalamic region, located just above the pituitary*

> *gland in the mid-brain, is 'wired' very uniquely for each of the sexes. Thus, the hypothalamus (known as the seat of the emotions) provides women with a different psychological frame of reference than that of men. Further, female sexual desire tends to be somewhat cyclical, correlated with the menstrual calendar, whereas males are acyclical.... Failure to understand this uniqueness can produce a continual source of marital frustration and guilt.* [1]

Yet, there is a real joy in this. As I have grown in my relationship with Valerie, those traits that make up her womanliness have rubbed off on me and made me both a better steward, a better husband, and a better worshipper of God. One day I watched her making coffee for breakfast. One moment it was a kind word for Nicole; at another, she picked her up and gave her a kiss. Next she prepared Nicole's cereal, cut up the peaches, and told a story to her as she did it. She even named the peach!

Now why is it, when I give Nicole breakfast, I push the bowl over, fill it up, and say, "Here"? Somehow it goes down better with all the frills. The womanly frills!

I am convinced that if we husbands will study our wives to learn those things about her God-given makeup as a woman, the profit will be immense. We will begin to see what it really means to be made together in the image of God.

In another of his books, *Straight Talk to Men and Their Wives,* Dobson lists several characteristics he finds unique to women. They are:

1. "A greater appreciation for stability, security, and enduring human relationships." Because of their concern for children and the family, women tend to be less willing to risk all in a daring business venture, or to take any step

that might lead to losing a house or one's basic physical security.

2. Her "emotional investment in her home . . . usually exceeds that of her husband." I personally discovered this once again when I decided to rearrange *my* office. I did it while Val was out—to surprise her! I put up some pictures, moved the shelving, and quietly placed the cabinets in one corner. When she arrived home, I was proud. But her first words were, "Ahhhh! What have you *done?*" By the time it was over, I'd rearranged it twice. But her arrangement was even better than mine!

When we first got married, Valerie moved into my apartment. Immediately, she began getting rid of all sorts of furniture and things I had lying about. It took her a while, but finally, she got things the way she wanted them. I asked why she didn't like it the way I had it. "Nothing matched," she said. "You had dust all over everything. In a word, it was junky."

Look, give me a sofa, a bed, and a table to eat from, and I'm content. In fact, you don't even have to keep the plates clean. Just pull one out of the sink and wash it off. But not a wife. She sees things much differently.

3. A basic "noncompetitive spirit." When we played "Trivial Pursuit" with some friends, they were not doing so well, and Val began giving them hints on the answers. Soon they were catching up to us. And I was getting mad. "Stop helping them get the answers," I said.

Val answered, "Come on. It makes it more fun when it's closer."

"I don't want it to be closer."

She laughed, and continued to give the hints despite my grumbling. Obviously, she saw the game as a chance to fellowship and have fun. I saw it as an opportunity to conquer!

4. "In how they develop self-esteem." Dobson suggests that men get their sense of worth from their job, being respected and successful in business. Women, however, and especially homemakers, "depend primarily on the romantic relationship with their husbands for ego support."

5. "The maternal instinct." Dobson suggests that this differs among women, but men are usually the ones who want to remain unattached and who fight the impulse to settle down. Most women want children and family sometime.

6. Finally, Dobson says that "the most dramatic differences between males and females are evident in their contrasting sexual preferences." Men tend to be more visual. Women, however, find their attraction to a particular man "with whom she has entered into an emotional relationship."[2]

More Differences

Yet, these are not all the elements that make men different from women. Here are a few more I have noted.

Feeling-oriented. Although there are always exceptions to the rule, I've noted that women tend to be more concerned about feelings and thoughts than actions. This isn't a criticism. It is just a totally different orientation for men. Male friends have said to me, "I don't understand it. I see a problem, I want to fix it. But my wife wants me to talk about it, to let out my feelings. Forget feelings; let's get moving." But a wife often wants you to understand her feelings before you move!

Dr. Gene Getz once amused his congregation by telling about a time when his young son, Kenton, wanted a puppy. Since the family already had a dog, Dr. Getz told him it would be too hard on the older dog. But Kenton kept whining and saying how nice it would be to have a puppy. Dr. Getz mustered all the force of his logic and demonstrated unequivocably why they *couldn't* take a puppy. When he finished, he felt like the proverbial blacksmith wiping his hands after a tough job. "Well, that finishes that!" But, his son was unconvinced.

Then his wife arrived on the scene, having listened from the kitchen. She knelt down by Kenton and said, "I bet the puppies were cute, weren't they?" He poured out his feelings, and after a few minutes concluded, "But I guess it wouldn't be fair to [the older dog] to bring in a young puppy." Mom agreed. With that, Kenton ran out to play, renewed and happy. Dr. Getz fixed his congregation with his eye and said whimsically, "Now, why can't I do that?"

Because you are a man. You're problem-oriented, not feeling-oriented. When you see a problem, you fix it. When your wife sees a problem, she wants to offer the person involved comfort, a pat, a word of encouragement, not an immediate solution.

A sense of drama. In general, men can get along fairly well with the humdrum, run-of-the-mill duties, getting the job done efficiently. The fewer the problems the better because he already has enough problems. That is not to say he does not enjoy excitement. But most of us would like to get a job done pronto and move on to the next without interruption.

I have noticed, though, that women like variety and change in life. This is not derogatory toward women. Frankly, it adds a lot. I know that I would probably settle down into the dust and never move again if my wife didn't stir things up now and then. We even know a couple in which the wife rearranges the living room at least once a month. We never knew how it would look when we visited. I asked her husband about it. He said, "She needs it to be different. She gets bored with the same old place."

Women desire romance, spice, a surprise, a change of pace now and then.

Verbal. For years, scores on SATs and the like have indicated that males do better on the mathematical part, but females consistently do better on the verbal. Many books on marriage mention the same thought. Wives tend to want to talk about a situation—their ideas, feelings, concerns.

I do not know how many times a husband has told me, "My wife's always saying I never talk to her anymore! I can't figure it out." Before the wedding, he was full of sweet nothings, tender words, great expectations, and hefty promises. But suddenly, after a few years, he seems to have run out of words.

A man who seeks to understand his wife will graciously seek to meet this need. Tell her what is on your heart. Share your problems. Let her know what is going on at work. Discuss your thoughts and goals. There is no such thing as the "strong, silent type." The fact is, these men just do not have much to say. The question is: Will they step out and begin to make themselves vulnerable with their wives? Or will they continue in silence—to the anger and detriment of all concerned?

Husband-oriented. I'm often amazed at what I overhear men and women talking about when I go to parties or socials. For men, it is sports or business or something in the political arena. But for the wives, it is often what their husbands are doing.

Wives, even those who work outside the home, center their lives on their husbands. It's the way God made them. Eve was Adam's "helpmate," one created specifically to meet *his* needs. Husbands should regard this as an attraction not a detraction, for it is the very thing that keeps a wife loyal, faithful, and helpful.

Just the same, a wife also wants to feel that her husband centers much of his life on her. Thus, a husband should communicate to his wife that he is thinking about her, too. A call from the office each day just to see how things are going is important. A flower every now and then, especially for no reason at all, communicates love and care. A note, hidden in some cupboard so she will find it as she works in the kitchen, can be a real lift. She needs to know that you do think about her, that you care, that you are deeply interested.

Sensitive. A wife's so called "sensitivity" has gotten a bad reputation. I have heard numerous times from many husbands that their wives are too sensitive. Somehow I doubt it. I think it's more likely that the husbands are too *in*sensitive.

A wife asks her husband as she models a new dress, "How do you like it?"

He looks up from the paper and says, "It's okay."

Suddenly, her smile fades. She leaves the room in a little huff, a little hurt.

The husband sits there and wonders, *Now what did I do?*

Ask yourself: how would you feel if you brought home a giant trout from a fishing trip, held it up for your wife, and said, "What do you think of this beauty?" and she answered, "It's okay"? Or, you just landed a big promotion and walked in the door with your new business card, "Vice President of Sales." You show it to her and say, "How do you like that, honey?" and she replies with a yawn, "Oh, that's nice."

The way you respond to her efforts at beauty and looking attractive to you is important. If you show indifference, is it any wonder she's upset? She is not being sensitive, as so many husband claim. No, you are just as sensitive—about the things important to you. We need to stop telling her she is too sensitive, and start thinking about how we would respond if she was callous about our ideas and joys.

Know Her as a Person

There is a second level in which we are to know her *as a person.* Of all the women on Planet Earth, I chose her. She is unique, and though she is all woman, she is different from all other women as well. Simply understanding the general characteristics of women is the beginning, but not the end, of marital bliss.

I have been learning that living with my wife in knowledge means that I seek to understand her as a person: what hurts her, what discourages her, what motivates her, what uplifts her. I need to know what she is sensitive about, what words upset her, and what actions comfort her. I am, in effect, to become a first rate student of my wife, observing everything I can about her. Why? Not only so that I can know her and better meet her needs, but also so that she can know me, and together we will discover the fullness of God's image.

In this respect, my wife constantly teaches me in areas where I have little or no understanding. I tend to be rather objective, always seeking to throw "perspective" into a situation. I always try to see a situation from everyone's point of view—except hers. That is a weakness of mine that I have to deal with daily. Loyalty to one's wife is vital. On this issue my wife has taught me much.

What characteristics do you, as her husband, recognize in your wife that make her unique and a complement to yourself? What traits do you, as his wife, want your husband to nurture and care about?

Ask yourself these questions:

1. If you believe God brought you and your wife together, what was His purpose? Could it be that she, as your complement, has strengths where you have weaknesses, and vice-versa?

2. If you believe that God has given your wife certain strengths where you have weaknesses, can you identify what they are? Sit down and discuss it with her.

3. If you believe God has joined you together to help you both grow into His image, what are you doing about it? Are you working together or against each other? Are you making her weaknesses reasons to fight, rather than reasons to grow?

My wife and I have put together a prayer file that includes cards citing areas of growth. Each of our weaknesses has received a special card in which we record growth and change. It is thrilling to see ourselves work together in this.

Live With Her as a Wife

A third aspect of living with our wives in an understanding way is knowing her *as a wife.* That special relationship between marriage partners can be shared by no one else. Seeing our wives as *women* helps us grow like a rose and a dandelion swaying together in a garden. When we begin to know her as a *person*, it is more like fitting together the pieces of a puzzle. We find that the fit is perfect and the picture beautiful. But knowing her as a *wife* plunges us into the depths of intimacy and all that marriage can offer. This is more than two flowers co-existing in a garden or a puzzle fitting together. It is the weaving of a fabric so fine that the threads of both lives lose themselves in each other. No longer are they sorting out strands. Rather, each life is seen as a unity, something that could never be torn without destroying the whole.

When we see our wives this way, we can begin to understand such things as her protectiveness toward the relationship, something many men find irksome. I have discovered that when my wife says of another woman, "She appears to be an exhibitionist," I had better listen. I tend to think people are just being nice, when there may be wrong motives involved. A wife will always react to anyone trying to establish intimacy with her husband because that is something for her alone.

We will also understand why she has such a strong desire for intimacy and the need for time together. One of our world's modern myths is that the quantity of time together is not as important as the quality. True. But you cannot get quality time without spending a quantity of time together. You can't spontaneously produce quality. It happens through the give and take of an intimate love relationship.

This is why our wives desire to share our dreams, hopes, fears, and depths of feeling. This is why "feelings" are so important to her. She wants to reach down and grasp those cords that ring the bells of our souls.

I realized this recently when I began withholding some problems from Val for fear that "she might not understand," or "her feelings might be hurt." But when I re-read in Scripture that we were to be one, I knew that I could not continue hiding those things from her. I had to share them so that she could enter into my deepest heart. When I began to share those feelings I had bottled up, an incredible release and security followed. There was nothing to hide between us, no secrets. I felt a comfort and a stability never realized before. I also sensed a level of acceptance and love that I never dreamed could occur. My wife and I had moved closer to truly becoming one flesh, one heart, and one mind.

Ask yourself if this is what you seek: intimacy, oneness, harmony? God says there is only one way to gain this. By living with our wives in knowledge—knowing her as a woman, as a person, and as a wife. When we do that, we will certainly touch every star God intends for our marriage.

[1] From *What Wives Wish Their Husbands Knew About Women* by James Dobson. Published by Tyndale House Publishers, Inc. © 1975. Used by permission.

[2] Our appreciation to Word Books for use of material from *Straight Talk to Men and Their Wives* by James Dobson.

—6—
Grant Her Honor

When Winston Churchill was Prime Minister of Great Britain, his marriage was considered one of the best examples in England of true loyalty and love. Often, when he gave a speech in the House of Commons, he would not begin until he had received a sign from her.

Later in his life, someone interviewed Mr. Churchill and asked, "If you could live again, what would you want to be?"

With a twinkle in his eye, Mr. Churchill replied, "Mrs. Churchill's next husband."

What a benediction on a marriage! And what a monumental compliment for one's wife.

Ask yourself for a moment: Would you say the same thing about your wife? If you wouldn't, it is probably not because of anything about her, but because of you. Maybe you simply are not offering her the honor and respect God commands. Wives want their husbands to place a high value on them, on marriage, and on making a good marriage.

Again, as we trek along through the commandments of God to husbands who seek to live in submission to Christ, we come to a second element found in Peter's bold statement to husbands. First Peter 3:7, "... Grant her honor as a fellow-heir of the grace of life, so that your prayers may not be hindered."

How then does a husband honor and love his wife the way our wedding vows idealized it? How does his submission to Christ work out in this area?

Grant Her Honor

Peter's expression, "grant her honor," comes from a Greek word which means "value" or "price." He is saying, "Value your wife, husband. Show her respect. Reverence her as your equal and partner in the presence of God."

This is the very principle many of us vowed at the altar. In this respect, I cannot help but think of how I treat those things I value: what I do with them; where I keep them; how I watch over them. One of my valued items are my computer diskettes. These contain multitudes of articles, poems, stories, and chapters for books. If a fire burned them up, or a soft drink was spilled on them, or someone stole them, thousands of hours of work would vanish. For that reason, I keep those diskettes in a safe place. I handle them gingerly. I buy the best diskettes and storage devices available. I keep a watchful eye on them, inspect them every day, make sure they are safe.

When I compare that to how we men occasionally treat our wives, I cringe. I have noticed the kinds of things we value by the way we talk. We say of our cars: "She's got four on the floor, overhead cam, mags, cream finish. She's a real beauty. Can I take you for a spin?" Our stamp collections: "I picked this set up on a trip to London. Man, I had to haggle with the fellow for twenty minutes just to get a reasonable price. But let me tell you, I got a bargain. This set is worth a mint!" Or our season seats at the ball park: "Wait 'til you see these, Joe. Right across from first base! You can get autographs from the players. I paid for them, but it was worth every penny."

But how do we talk about our wives to others? What special treatment do we give them that shows how important they are to us?

As I reflect on my own marriage, I have seen at least four ways that I am learning to honor my wife.

By Communicating Commitment

Commitment is not a dirty word nowadays. Pastors talk about it. Husbands affirm it. But do we really understand it?

I tend to think of commitment as a deep down conviction that I will stick with my wife through everything. That is true. But it is the working out of that "sticking" which often eludes us. Am I committed enough to pray for my wife's needs daily and spend time discussing them? When in the heat of marital disagreement, can I avoid making threats? Am I willing to work through problems, plugging away until real change is observed?

Commitment is expressed primarily by what we do, not only when things are tough, but in the daily wrangle and tangle of life. Here are some examples of ways to show commitment:

- By expressing love and encouragement even when you would rather read the paper.
- By listening and responding even when you are ready for bed.
- By offering to help with the household work though you would rather collapse onto the sofa.
- By eliminating threats and the word "divorce" from your vocabulary.
- By controlling your anger even when the fuse is lit.
- By working at communication and change.
- By spending time in the Word and prayer together.
- By reading books together and seeking to develop the relationship.

One of the real breakthroughs in this area comes through learning "to speak the truth in love." It is so easy to manipulate, to try to get the other to do what you wish without coming out and saying it plainly. But Val and I have recently come to a mutual commitment to speak what we feel and mean without trying to "trick" the other into doing it our way.

For instance, I asked my wife, "Would you like to listen to so-and-so tonight on the radio?"

She replied, "Do you?"

I said, "Whatever you want to do." But suddenly I realized I was leaving the burden and decision up to her. Instantly, I reversed gears and said, "Look, I'd like to listen to him. Would you care to join me and listen together? I'd like you to."

It is a small thing. But I've found that such truth-telling touches nearly everything we say. It takes commitment to keep working at it. The joy is that such commitment gives us the ability to share our feelings on deeply sensitive issues that we used to tiptoe around.

Still, you don't communicate commitment simply by

saying, "I'm committed to you." You do it by actions. Things like courtesy. Do you still play the role of the gentleman with your wife, or are you "beyond" all that? "Let her open the door. She's able."

It is a thrill for me to watch an elderly couple in our church as they walk down the aisle to their pew. They are always holding hands. He will often put his arm around her as they listen and worship. Couples do not have to express public affection. Some are more reticent than others. The point is, is there affection? Is love communicated?

This struck me very significantly one Sunday as my wife and I stood to sing a hymn. I held the book, but I noticed my wife wasn't singing. When we sat down, I sensed a distance. I wrote her a note. "What's wrong?"

She wrote back that she was feeling hurt. After the service I asked her what was going on. It turned out that she felt I had been withholding affection from her because of a mishap that morning.

I thought through what had happened and realized how I had given her the "silent treatment" on our drive to church because of that mishap. I had led her to see everything that I did as me punishing her. It was disrespectful and unkind. Immediately I told her I would never withhold affection to punish her, and that if I was angry about something, I would tell her right away—not give her the silent treatment. It's a small thing, but it can knock down big walls when the relationship is hurting.

Fidelity Within and Without

A second aspect of granting our wives honor comes under the heading of *fidelity*. This, again, is one of those wedding vow words that is not too hard to obey outwardly, even though our age seems to be italicized with the words adultery, fornication, perversion, and lasciviousness.

Granting my wife honor in this area goes much deeper, though. One day Val remarked to me, "You think so-and-so is pretty, don't you?" I didn't want to provoke anything so I just said, "No." She replied, "Yes, you do. I could tell by the way you looked at her."

She let it drop, but I realized my heart was not right. It is too easy in our day to feed on the pictures that assault our minds from billboards, magazines (even the decent ones), paperback novels, and even people walking about scantily clad. When we let our eyes wander, we not only wound our wives, but, in effect, reject them. I am finding that fidelity means I reserve certain looks only for my wife and her body. And I don't lie to her. Thus, I flip past the model photos in *TIME* a little more quickly and keep a tight reign on my thoughts, letting nothing intrude that might begin an unholy desire.

One night at my in-laws' house, we were watching a variety show and suddenly the screen filled with writhing bodies in skintight outfits. I calmly covered my eyes and said to Val, "Tell me when it's over."

She laughed and shook her head. But her sister suddenly asked, "What's wrong, Mark? Can't you even watch a few people dancing?"

I replied, "I don't need any pictures like that in my mind."

She shot a few more barbs at me, but Val came to my defense. "I appreciate it, honey." Val's mom said, "Mark, you're one in a million."

It felt good to have them respect what I was doing. Other wives have told me that our world is difficult enough without having your husband making you feel like you have to compete against million dollar models with touched up faces and flawless figures.

Fidelity must be cultivated. Job said that he made a "covenant with his eyes," not to gaze on women (Job 31:1). It takes effort and real marital commitment not to gape, gawk, or lust at other women. But if your wife sees you doing that, it will produce in her insecurity, anger, and resentment.

Respect

A third idea that comes out of Peter's thought here is *respect.* Any man who does not respect his wife cannot possibly honor her, for respect is the essence and foundation of honor.

And, again, respect is a loose abstraction that must be brought down into the concrete of daily life. Some of the ways to give our wives greater respect is by:

- listening to her opinions with an open mind;
- making her feel special in the presence of others, especially by the way I speak of her to them;
- including her in all decisions that affect us together;
- the way I handle money.

This last area—the way I handle our money—has hit me recently with fresh insight. I had been praying that the Lord would teach me to respect and love my wife better. One day while I was writing the checks, including the one I give her for her expenses, I suddenly realized that I regarded the money I gave to the church as somehow having greater importance than what I gave her. I thought that while God was very pleased with what I gave Him through the church, the money I gave her was more like the wood, hay, and stubble of I Corinthians 3. It just did not count in the eyes of God. As a result, there was a twinge of resentment with every dollar I had to give her.

That is when the Spirit of God struck. He convicted me that this attitude was totally wrong. In fact, as I studied Scripture on it and prayed about it, I realized that money given to anyone or anything out of love and concern for real need was as sacred and worthy of eternal reward as anything given to the church. "If any one does not provide for his own, and especially for those of his household, he has denied the faith, and is worse than an infidel." First Timothy 5:8 hit home, and this insight transformed my whole attitude. Suddenly, I was able to give money to my wife with the same joy that I gave to the church. I began to treat her with new and greater respect.

A man also shows respect for his wife about her work. One woman lamented to me that she felt utterly rejected by her husband. "Why?" I asked. She was an industrious person with a lovely home which she cared for exquisitely.

"He doesn't think much of me since I'm just a housewife."

I probed further and discovered that he repeatedly put her down about the fact that anyone could do housewife chores. It took brains, however, to do the kind of work he did.

That husband was conducting a modern version of the ancient art of water torture. Each drop of sarcasm had burned into his wife's psyche until she felt like little more than a zero.

Respect also comes in the way we husbands treat our wives about their work in the home. Do we see such work as beneath us, and therefore she should do it all? Or are we willing to help, even if only a little on Saturdays?

I remember reading a short article about a mountain

man who was visited by a social worker. His wife was laboring out in the garden under a broiling sun. The social worker queried, "Kind of hot out there. Your wife do that all day?"

"Naw," said the mountain man, "we work in shifts."

"Oh, you mean after she gets tired, you go out and work in the garden?"

"Naw, when she gits tired in the garden, then I have her come in and do the house chores."

Our world classifies certain things as "women's work" and others as "men's work." But there is the need today for a meeting of the 'mines.' No longer, "This work is mine, and that's yours," but, "let's do it together until it's done."

I have produced a few moments of wide-eyed astonishment from my wife when I've hauled myself up from the couch and volunteered to do a chore without her asking. I hope I produce more in the days ahead.

Trust

A fourth element of granting honor comes through the word *trust.* If there is no trust between partners, there is no real sharing or mingling of souls. They have not given themselves to one another unconditionally.

Trust has many elements: keeping confidences, speaking the truth in love, maintaining your commitments (such as getting home on time), and informing one another of your plans and actions. But two areas I have given high priority are how I speak of my wife before others, and how I deal with those who may complain to me about her.

Any couple has secrets, weaknesses, foibles, and problems that we don't want others to know about. It is not necessarily because we are ashamed, but there are many things that should be kept inside the relationship. Otherwise, trust is compromised and intimacy ends. It has been a difficult lesson for me because I tend to think that any illustration from my life that might help another should be shared. Why hide it? But I have come to see that a husband cannot operate that way. He must be careful what he shares with others.

One night years ago, at a family gathering, I told a joke about my wife that I thought was very funny. But my uncle did not laugh. He only replied, "Boy, do you have a lot to learn." I noticed my wife was not laughing either.

It was an important lesson. But the rule of thumb might be, if there is any question about whether or not to tell this information, joke, story, etc., it probably should not be shared.

The converse of that is consciously sharing good things about your wife in the presence of others. For several years now I have been cultivating the habit of telling others how wonderful my wife is—especially in her presence. Recently I got off the bandwagon and stopped talking. Val noticed. She asked me, "How come you so rarely say anything nice about me to others like you used to?"

Frankly, I hadn't noticed.

"Yes, you hardly ever say anything. In fact, you don't even show me much affection when you're around other people."

Suddenly, I realized that around certain people, I tended to be a little more reserved about these things. I had followed their lead. But it was important to Val that I not only communicate to her before others, but also send the same message to them: "I love my wife!"

Another whole area is how we deal with those who may

complain to us about our spouses. Occasionally, someone has voiced some criticism of my wife. In the past, I would listen, and then go to her trying to find out what the problem was. Often I seemed to be on the critic's side and accusatory. As a result, my wife felt our trust was broken. I was not supporting her or being loyal the way I should.

I have found that telling such critics to talk to my wife about their complaint usually ends the matter. When people persist, I tell them I won't listen, and walk away. That has become a critical juncture in my own spiritual life, for it taught me not only how to handle such criticism, but how to maintain my loyalty.

Do You Want Your Prayers Answered?

Finally, granting our wives honor is critical not only to our marital health but also to our spiritual heath. Peter says if we are not practicing this, our prayers will be hindered. This covers the whole range from not wanting to pray, to God not answering.

This becomes a barometer of our spiritual life. Are your prayers answered? If not, then maybe you are not treating your wife right! Take inventory. Give your treatment of her a hard look. Ask her outright: Do you think I'm showing respect for you, being loyal, and building trust? If not, why not? Open yourself up to her comments. It could be not only a revelation, but a rejuvenation to your marital life.

—7—
Love as Christ Loved

It all started with a slice of pepperoni pizza. I had been praying for several days that the Lord would teach me to love my wife as Christ loved the church. I had not seen much action yet. (I guess I was waiting for the *Lord* to do something.) Valerie and I had decided on a quiet evening of intimate talk, a little television, and pizza. A local service dropped the food by, and as Val prepared some soft drinks in the kitchen, I carved out two slices and put them on our plates. Then, as I listened to the news, I suddenly noticed her slice had three more pepperonis than mine.

I gazed hungrily at that hearty slice teeming with pepperonis and listened for her in the kitchen. She was still getting the drinks. Suddenly, I made my choice and quickly made an exchange. "She'll never know," I told myself.

Then the Lord hit me. "What was that request about your wife you were praying this week?"

Instant conviction. "But my wife's not into pepperonis, Lord!"

I tried to shake it off, but the Lord was absolutely persistent. Finally, I decided to make another switch. When she came in and sat down, she had no idea that a battle had just been fought. And won!

Somehow I felt good and clean inside. I felt that I had made real strides in learning to love my wife as Christ loved the church.

Well, maybe not strides, but baby steps anyway.

A Big Lesson

It was an important lesson. I did not expect the Lord to answer the way He did. I tend to think that sacrifices for my wife involve things like asking to be shot in her place when the terrorists come by the house. Or, getting run over by the car as I leap to knock her out of the way while crossing the street. At least, that is the way I had always imagined it. Something with drama. Flair. Something stupendous. Not giving up a slice of pepperoni pizza!

Yet, I am finding that sacrifice—realistic, consistent "giving yourself up for her"—involves the little things much more than any incredible act of courage.

That is nearly so obvious one tends to smile. "You mean you didn't know that?"

Frankly, no. Yet, it is the essence of the submissive man's outlook. If we are to love our wives as Christ loved the church, we must begin to "give ourselves up" for them.

I was married on February 14, 1983, three days after the monster snowstorm of that year. We were actually supposed to be married on the 12th, but the weatherman did not warn us far enough ahead of time about this 36 incher that would blow in on the 11th.

I was 32 years old and ready. Also, self-centered, egotistical, habituated to my lifestyle, and totally unaware of the responsibility and changes that marriage would bring. But I believed Val was my Eve and when she came into my life, I was saying with Adam, "This is my other half!"

In light of that, I began asking God to lead us into a pure and passionate marriage, though not necessarily a perfect one. We began studying Ephesians 5:22-33. Her part was easy for me. "Just follow my leadership," I told Val. "That's what Paul was saying."

But she wanted to know more about verses 25 and 26: "Husbands, love your wives just as Christ also loved the church and gave Himself up for her; that He might sanctify her . . . . " "What's this about 'giving yourself' up for me?" she asked.

"Well," I said, with some clearing of the throat. "It means that I'm supposed to sacrifice myself for you like Jesus did on the cross."

"How?"

Why did she have to get down to the nitty-gritty like that? Couldn't we just leave it in those flaming, idealistic terms that glowed in the dark but seemed so hard to grasp in the light?

No.

"So how do you sacrifice for me?"

"You know. Like if you needed a new kidney, I would volunteer to give you one of mine."

Right. I decided to gently veer off the subject.

But it bothered me. How *was* I supposed to "give myself up" for her? I asked the Lord to give me insight. And over the next few months He did!

As I said, I first became aware of it with that pepperoni pizza. But that was not the end. One night as I was preparing her an iced tea in the kitchen, I dropped an ice cube on the floor. Now, the way I think may be perverse, but I just plopped the floored ice cube back into her glass. It was then that a voice deep down inside me uttered a favorite phrase, "Is that the loving thing to do for your wife?"

I decided to take the cube out, broke out another ice tray, and was about to add one last cube when the still, small voice said again, "By the way, when you put the ice from the floor into the glass, you contaminated the glass and the other ice cubes. Right?"

I was immediately chagrined. "Oh, come on," I argued with that inner voice, "you mean I have to get a whole new glass and ice cubes?"

"That's not the question. The question is, 'Do you want to love your wife as Christ loved the church?' "

"Okay," I said, and I did it right. But something within me laughed. "You know, Lord, I didn't realize what a selfish lout I was until you started waking me up!"

One Saturday morning, I woke up and wandered into the kitchen half comatose, only to notice that I had left a mess from the night before. But I had told myself, "That's her job." This morning, a voice inside me said, "I think this is your job, friend."

He was right. I did the dishes. And I was even smiling when Val got up and sauntered in, although she nearly collapsed when she realized what I was doing.

Another time, when our daughter was about seven months old, I remember her waking up at 3 a.m., crying for a bottle. Val wheezed in her sleep, "Do you think you could feed her this time?"

I tried to feign deep sleep, but she shook me and said louder, "Hey, do you think *you* could feed her this time?" Again, the actor in me arose. I said, "Huh? What?" And rolled over with a loud, pretend snore.

Val was not to be daunted. She poked me again, "Hey, Mark! WILL YOU FEED NICOLE, PLEASE?!" I sat up, still pretending, when the Lord spoke to me. "Mark, are you loving your wife the way you should?" Immediately, I staggered out to Nicole's bedroom.

As I fed the baby that early morning, I began to realize that this was another way to sacrifice. In general, we men are highly unconscious of the ways we take our wives for granted. We fail to make the little sacrifices because we think of ourselves first. The monumental sacrifices may come along only once in a lifetime. It is the daily, small acts in between which receive minor to major action depending on our real willingness to give that show if we are loving in the way Christ intends.

How To Sacrifice

How, then, can we men become more sacrificial toward our wives, giving not only with joy but with style?

1. *Ask the Lord for insight into your selfishness and lack of sacrifice.* That is a dangerous prayer because He will do it. He will knock down all your self-satisfied images of your actions with His searing revelations. But that is the place to start.

Let me share something that happened to me. Then, look within yourself and analyze your relationship.

One night as we were going out to dinner, I was making suggestions about several places. Val mentioned only one place she wanted to go. I quickly brushed it aside and suggested several others. She mentioned her spot again.

But I shook my head and said, "Probably a long wait." Suddenly, Val said, "Don't you want to go where I want to go?"

"But that place always has such a big crowd. We'll have to wait an hour. And anyway these other places are close by and . . . . "

"They're a lot cheaper," she said angrily.

Oh, that hurt. "Cheaper!" I nearly shouted. "Is that all this is? You just want me to take you to an expensive place?"

"That would be nice. For once."

We drove a little further and suddenly it hit me. I turned to my wife. "Valerie, I'm sorry. I am acting like a tightwad. Will you forgive me?"

She smiled and nodded as I turned in the direction of her restaurant.

It's a big problem, though, with many men. We just don't want to spend the extra dollar. So we finagle for the cheaper place and lose every way around.

Ask yourself:

Do we always go where I want to go?

Do I only give in to her after a fight? Or almost a fight?

Do I ever initiate taking her to a place she likes?

Does she have to beg me to do something special, even flowers?

If your answer is yes to any of the above, take a hard look at yourself. You're selfish!

2. *Study the ways Jesus gave Himself up for the church.* What did Jesus do? Some of the ways were:

After a long day of healing and preaching, He still found the time to heal Peter's mother-in-law and numerous others that evening (Matthew 8:14-17).

He touched the leper, willing to make Himself unclean for another's good.

He held the children and warned His disciples not to hinder them from coming to Him.

He spoke the truth even though He knew others might react with anger.

He made Himself vulnerable by opening Himself up to His disciples.

He shared His inner self with them—and us in the pages of Scripture.

He repeatedly found time for those who were hurting and suffering even when His own disciples would have dragged Him away from them.

He took time for inquirers, like Nicodemus, even when they came to Him timidly and secretly.

He reached out even though He had overwhelming needs (the woman at the well).

He remained loyal to His disciples even though He knew they would desert Him in the final hours of His life.

Though He never criticized people for their weaknesses, He confronted them about their sins.

He starts with us where we are, not where we should be.

He suffered the humiliation, pain, and degradation of the cross.

He lives even now to intercede for us and lead us to glorify the Father.

Any one of these truths can be applied to your marriage.

3. *Pray that the Holy Spirit will point out opportunities for you to give of yourself.* Again, a serious prayer. The Lord will do it. He created us for good works, and this is just one of the type He longs to lead us into (Ephesians 2:10).

An interesting thing happened to me one afternoon. I was taking my daily walk through a local mall at lunchtime. A survey organization had a lady posted in my path, and I decided to give her a tract. Immediately, she wanted to know if I would go through the survey. She added the clincher when she said, "This takes about 15 minutes, so we're willing to pay you three dollars to do it."

That was fine with me.

That night I happened to go by the grocery store on an errand and discovered the three dollars still in my pocket. What should I do with it? Instantly, the still small voice had an answer. *Why not get your wife a couple of red baby roses on a lark?* I picked out two, used my three dollars, and won my wife's heart once again.

This is not anything particularly astonishing. But if a man will let the Lord speak to his heart and his imagination, He'll supply him with numerous surprises, treasures, and gifts to act on day in and day out.

4. *Ask yourself each day, "How can I do something special for my wife today?"* It takes discipline, but I find that it is a habit which pays high dividends. I have been trying to do one special thing for my wife every day. It takes a conscious effort. But it adds a special glow to my day, and also warms an embrace. What kinds of things?

An extra long kiss and hug.

A note hidden in the cupboard.

Her favorite candy bar wrapped with a bow.

A special word of encouragement.

A card for no reason but that you love her.

Volunteering to wash the dishes, vacuum the floor, or do some other task she might not like.

A special evening with a special show and your arm over her shoulder.

Volunteer to make some popcorn.

A special time of prayer or Bible study.

A walk, hand in hand.

Use your creativity. There are multitudes of things. All it takes is some prayer, some thought, and a determination to follow through.

5. *Start doing those things that come to mind.* This is an obvious point, but often missed. You can't just think about what you'll do. You have to do it! It is too easy to lie around and chuckle to yourself about some scheme, and then never actually do it.

On the other hand, making the effort to accomplish your actions inundates a home with joy.

One of the best Christmas gifts a friend ever gave his wife was an idea he got from an article he found in *Reader's Digest* written by Taylor Caldwell. She spoke of how her husband, with the greatest of secrecy, hid himself away in a room and made her a special gift. It was a bottle full of little pieces of colored paper. When she opened them up, one said, "This good for one stint by me at the sink washing dishes." Another, "This good for one movie." Another, "This good for one night out."

That jolted my thinking. One year I tied notes around a miniature candy cane—to sweeten it a little. Another year, I wrote up actual checks, each good for a special date, a night out, a movie, a restaurant meal, a show, a baseball game. I found that these little gifts of love not only showed I cared, but also gave Val an opportunity to look forward to some things we might do together in the year ahead.

6. *Don't worry if she doesn't appear to notice at first.* Pat and Jill Williams have catalogued some of their trials as a married couple in their book, *Rekindled.* Pat had become so embroiled in his work that he allowed his wife to spin

through an emotional ringer that left her devastated and burned out. She came to the point where she did not care about him, their marriage, or anything else. In a confrontation in which Jill leveled with him about her feelings, Pat was leveled! But he sprang into action through the counsel of a book by Dr. Ed Wheat. In it, Dr. Wheat spelled out an acrostic that he said could rekindle any flickering marriage. The acrostic was B-E-S-T. "B" was for "bless." "E" was for "edify." "S" equalled "share," and "T," "touch."

In these principles, Pat Williams saw new hope and began seeking to bless, edify, share with, and touch his wife.

But for over two weeks, Jill showed no signs of life, or that she noticed any of Pat's new efforts. Many of us would give up after one or two tries, thinking, "She didn't even notice my best efforts, so why should I try again?" But that cannot be the attitude. We do what is loving even if the other does not notice or respond. Isn't that the essence of obedience to Christ?

Fortunately for Pat Williams, his wife did respond. In a few short weeks their marriage was rekindled with new life. I would recommend their book heartily. And also the "B-E-S-T" formula.

But others may not get so quick an answer. What matters is that we keep trying, hoping that our spouse will catch the spirit and the heart of it all.

7. *Repeat these actions and attitudes until they become the pattern of your life.* My seminary roommate used to tell me, "You have to keep on keeping on." It's a cliché, but that's the essence of it. Hang tough. Stay strong. Stand firm. Don't give in. Keep on truckin'! When the going gets tough, the tough get going. We have a million expressions. But it is not the words that count. It is the actions.

How Do You Feel?

I can almost see you sagging in your seat. "Man, Mark, this is tough stuff. You mean God expects me to do all this?"

Yes. And more we will look at in the pages ahead.

But let me offer a word to the wives. Remember to be patient. God isn't through with your husband yet. It will take time. Many of us men have blinders on our eyes as thick as the sides of a super-hardened missile silo. But the Lord will work. Pray for your husband. Watch. Wait. One day he may offer you the best strawberry in the bowl. And not even make a big deal about it!

—8—
Sanctify Her

What is Christ's purpose in salvation? Is it simply that we might be happy, have eternal life, and go to heaven?

No. It is much more. It is that He might make us like Himself—holy, blameless, above reproach, perfect (Romans 8:29; Philippians 1:6; I Peter 2:5,9,21).

Husbands are to have the same purpose in relation to their wives. Ephesians 5:25-27 further commands, "Husbands, love your wives, just as Christ also loved the church and gave Himself up for her; that He might sanctify her, having cleansed her by the washing of water with the word, that He might present to Himself the church in all her glory, having no spot or wrinkle or any such thing; but that she should be holy and blameless." Just as Christ wants to present the church to Himself "in all her glory . . . holy and blameless," so a husband must consider his goal the sanctity and godliness of his wife.

His giving and sacrifice is not designed simply to satisfy her. His effort in edifying and leading her is not simply a tactic to keep the peace. It all works together to produce holiness in the life of the wife.

Too Much of a Load?

Some would object here, saying, "I can't sanctify my wife; that's the Lord's job." Or, "You're laying a huge burden on husbands. How can they make their wives holy? No human can make another human blameless in God's eyes."

Correct. But what we are talking about is the husband's purpose, his goal, where his efforts are leading. He is not interested in merely holding his marriage together. Simply "making it work" is not the desire of his heart. Nor it is his wife's happiness. Rather, their relationship ought to be one that enhances spirituality, develops godliness, and encourages holiness. While true sanctification is a sovereign work of the Holy Spirit, His means is people, husbands included. "We proclaim Him, admonishing every man and teaching every man with all wisdom, that we may present every man complete in Christ" (Colossians 1:28). Every husband has a part in his wife's development as a Christian, and the wife has a role in her husband's sanctification.

What Is Sanctification?

Sanctify means to "make holy," to "separate for special use." In your household you may have certain utensils or china used only on special occasions. They are reserved for "special use." Sanctification means that we are selected out of the world for special use by the Lord. Becoming a Christian is like being plucked out of a normal Washington, D.C. job and becoming the President's special secretary and helper. You no longer perform according to your former job description; you do what the President says. Even more so, a sanctified person sets himself apart for the Lord's exclusive use. Just as a sergeant does not question his captain's command, so a saint ("sanctified one") refuses to question his Lord; he obeys.

Scripture presents sanctification, however, at several different levels. There is a primary sense which we often call *positional* sanctification. When we became Christians, we transferred from one position to another. As non-Christians, we sat in an electric chair. We were only waiting for Death to flip the switch. As Christians, we were moved to a throne. God placed us in His mansion on Eternity Street. We changed positionally. It has nothing to do with feelings or actions. It happened the instant we believed in Christ regardless of our time/space situation.

On the other hand, there is *practical* sanctification. This has everything to do with condition. This is the sense in which we have actually attained to a measure of holiness. A Christian grows. He changes. The Spirit transforms him. He lives differently from the way he used to live. He is a "new creature," and he begins acting out that new creature-likeness.

Living up to Christ's name is what practical sanctification is about. Positionally we are saved. But practically, we can sin. It is like focusing a slide on a projector. The slide itself is our position in Christ. It is perfect. But the Spirit has to take away the fuzziness, the blurs, the imperfections. The process of sanctification is where the Spirit seeks to bring us into focus to the original picture—Christ.

Unfortunately, that is a lifelong process. No Christian, living in an earthly body, will cease to sin. But when

Christ joins our spirits to our spiritual bodies at the rapture of the church, we will undergo the third stage of sanctification, *permanent* sanctification. This is when the image of Christ in us merges so that we become perfectly and permanently like Him.

A husband's task, then, is to contribute his part to the process of practical sanctification in his wife. He gives the Holy Spirit room to work through him. And the wife is to do the same with him. How, then, can a husband contribute to the sanctification of his wife?

Add, Don't Subtract

The first thing a husband should do is add to his wife's holiness, not subtract from it. His life, example, and influence should not drag her down, but should lift her up.

Mark Twain's wife, Lidy, was a Christian when they were married. Twain even made an effort in their first days of marriage to go to church. However, during the long years of his atheism and invective against the church, he chipped away at her faith. Later in their lives, during a time of grief, Twain took an about-face and told her that she should find solace in her faith. She replied, "I can't, Mark, I can't." Twain's influence had destroyed her ability to exercise her faith.

There are a multitude of ways a fleshly husband drags his wife down. One is simply through a poor example. If he indulges in godless activities, his wife will soon follow his lead.

One area in which I have struggled comes out of the video revolution. I found that numerous Christian friends would recommend certain movies, even those rated "R," saying, "Oh, it's fun," and "there's nothing really terrible in it." As a result, movies that I would never see in the theater, I'd watch on cassette. It became a practice to watch "popular" movies at home even though they contained violence, filthy speech, and nudity. What I found was that I could not easily dislodge certain images from my mind once they had taken root. More than once my mind has echoed words I had heard on the screen and that I thought I'd wiped from my memory. But when I heard my three-year-old repeat a phrase she had heard in one of our "PG" movies, that was the end. I knew I was not contributing to anyone's sanctification, much less my own.

Satan is subtle. He works best on the slight downhill grade, not the cliff. As Peter says, "Be of sober spirit, be on the alert. Your adversary, the devil, prowls about like a roaring lion, seeking someone to devour" (I Peter 5:8).

Another arena comes in the area of reading. As an aspiring writer of fiction, I began to rationalize the necessity to read so called "popular fiction," saying I needed to know what was out there and why it did so well. In a magazine, I read that a certain book was a "classic," and thought if that was so, I ought to read it. But when a relative saw me reading it, she asked, "Isn't that kind of a dirty book?" I responded about my discovery that it was a "classic." She just said, "It's a classic because it was one of the first mass circulation novels that got away with explicit sex." I had not reached any bad parts yet, but I decided not to continue reading. I knew that if I compromised in those areas, the rest of my family would follow. It also occurred to me that this "classic" business was just another one of Satan's euphemisms for sin.

Still another area is drinking. Every now and then I enjoyed having a little wine with dinner. That soon led to a glass every Friday night. When I found myself actually looking forward to it one day, I realized it had taken hold. I needed to stop.

These are all areas in which some Christians have overreacted, saying such prohibitions are legalism. But what we have seen in our day, through our reaction to past legalisms, is virtual license. In our desire to show we are not Pharisees, we have gone to the other side and become libertines!

A husband's example, though, extends to far more than just movies, books, and alcohol. What about the whole area of his speech around the house? When you are in a fight, do you resort to coarse language or harsh put-downs? What kinds of things do you talk about, revel in? If your son notices you ogling thinly clad figures on the television screen, what will he think and be tempted to do? All sorts of sins—prejudice, hatred, slander, gossip, lust—are learned through observation. A husband who indulges in these things could quickly lead not only his wife, but his whole family into sin.

On the opposite side of the coin of example is repentance, confession, forgiveness. What kind of attitude do you display when you make mistakes, even sin? Is it one of repentance, heartfelt contrition, and specific confession before the Lord?

One evening as my wife and I prayed by our couch, I took some time to confess sin. But what I confessed was very general. I prayed, "Lord, please forgive me for the mistakes I've made and help me do better." Afterward Valerie said, "I thought you were supposed to be specific when you confessed sin." Instant conviction. Actually I had been aware of some things I'd done to her, but I did not want to confess them specifically because she would know what I meant. However, when I decided to make a real confession, I was set free. We rejoiced together afterward. The frayed towlines were spiritually reknotted.

Take the Initiative in Spiritual Things

Paul makes an interesting statement in I Timothy 2:8: "Therefore I want the men in every place to pray, lifting up holy hands, without wrath and dissension." Occurring, as it does, in the context of both a woman's and a man's behavior in the church, I find it fascinating. Why did he add that little phrase, "without wrath and dissension"?

Having participated in a multitude of prayer meetings, I think I know why. Men sometimes consider being demonstrative in church services with a "not me" attitude. In any meeting I've been in, it seems the women are much more eager to pray, and to pray with zeal and passion, than men. They are much more reserved. I think it has something to do with our condition as a result of the Fall. Remember that Eve was deceived. She may have thought she was doing good by eating the forbidden fruit. But Adam knew better. He rebelled.

That rebellious streak continues today. Men know better, but they often fail to take the initiative in spiritual things in the home. It is Mom who teaches the kids to pray, Mom who leads devotions, and Mom who sits down with the Bible and methodically instructs the children. Dad is reading the paper, mowing the yard, or watching sports on TV.

But taking the lead in spiritual matters is critical to the sanctification of the husband and wife.

Charlie Shedd again provides potent help in his book, *Letters to Karen.* In spiritual matters he recommends:

> *1. Make a compact that you will set aside some time each day when you look Godward together.*

2. Select some devotional guide which suits you.

3. When your appointed time has come, you sit together quietly while one of you reads the day's selection.

4. Now you talk over what you would like to pray about. If Vincent is concerned with something in his business, he may appreciate the opportunity to tell you this. Perhaps you will confess that he hurt your feelings this morning, and you haven't been able to put that where it belongs. You may ask for clarification, if you need it, but you will not argue. You simply place before each other things which are on your hearts. [1]

You may disagree with the mechanics, but the process is basically sound. As you finish by holding hands and praying together that special time of God consciousness magnetizes the marital relationship. Many problems are cleared up simply by getting into the spiritual battle together.

Moses' word to the Israelites in the book of Deuteronomy still speaks to us today. He told them,

Hear, O Israel! The Lord is our God, the Lord is one! And you shall love the Lord your God with all your heart and with all your soul and with all your might. And these words, which I am commanding you today, shall be on your heart; and you shall teach them diligently to your sons and shall talk of them when you sit in your house and when you walk by the way and when you lie down and when you rise up. And you shall bind them as a sign on your hand and they shall be as frontals on your forehead. And you shall write them on the doorposts of your house and on your gates (6:4-9).

We do not have signs on our hands and frontals on our forehead today. But Moses' command still speaks to us. He was trying to lead the people into making worship, holiness, and walking with God the pattern of their lives. Every aspect of life was to be soaked with heavenly dew. Anyone who came by would instantly recognize, "These people are followers of Jehovah."

What do people notice when they come to your home? Many of the plaques and things people put up on walls may be religious "jargon;" and certainly we are not to wear placards as we walk to the office. But what magazines would one likely find on your table? Would a Bible be evident? Would someone who ate dinner with you notice anything different about your prayer of thanks? Would your conversation feature flashes of faith, a little spiritual experience shared as part of the dinner?

What Moses commanded was that fathers take spiritual charge of their households. When they rose and when they headed for bed, when they sat by the path and walked on the sidewalk, their speech, manner, and lives were to be filled with reverence and love for God.

God's Word teaches repeatedly that a man is to be the head of his home in spiritual matters. When Dad isn't, godliness soon gets waylaid and takes second place—to everything else.

If you are struggling with taking the reins of leadership in this area, consider several things:

1. If your wife knows more than you about the Bible, don't despair. She can give her input. You simply take the initiative.

2. Don't force everything into a mold. It is good to have a special time each evening, but try to give it variety. Use different devotionals, Christian magazine articles, or the words of a favorite hymn in addition to specific Scripture passages. Be creative.

3. Spend time on your own in study. Watch television less and give less time to personal activities. Give Jesus your best.

4. Find a support group of men who might provide extra insight in these matters. I meet with a group from "Christian Businessmen's Committee" (CBMC). These men have provided much help and counsel in my Christian walk.

5. Don't give up just because your "quiet time" is a little dull at first. There will always be dry times, even with lifelong practitioners. Persevere.

6. Pray that the Holy Spirit will give you "variations on the theme." He will spark new ideas you would never get from a magazine or group.

7. Learn to take advantage of the moment. Ask the Lord to provide spiritual insight about everyday things. Object lessons. Analogies. Stories. Illustrations. Look for practical application of spiritual truths.

All it takes is a man who will try in the power of the Spirit.

Speak the Truth in Love

Several times in this book I have referred to "speaking the truth in love." It is a critical item in the list of principles that sanctify a home and relationship. Just what is it, and what can it do?

Paul uses the phrase in Ephesians 4:14-15: "As a result, we are no longer to be children, tossed here and there by waves, and carried about by every wind of doctrine, by the trickery of men, by craftiness in deceitful scheming; but speaking the truth in love, we are to grow up in all aspects into Him, who is the head, even Christ." Paul applies the same idea a little later in verse 25: "Therefore, laying aside falsehood, speak truth, each one of you, with his neighbor, for we are members of one another."

Notice several facts.

- Without the truth, we are likely to be tossed about everywhere, never able to set down roots or stand firm.
- The purpose of speaking the truth in love is to help us grow up into the image of Christ.
- What we are to speak is "truth," reality—that which is right in God's eyes.
- We are to do it "in love," with gentleness, compassion, patience, and understanding, not beating one another with it.
- We speak truth because we are spiritually connected—"members" of one another. Not telling the truth to your wife is like shooting yourself in the eye.

The primary way a couple grows spiritually comes through each speaking truth to the other. Do not classify this with nagging or criticism. It is not the same thing. It is a different brand of speech altogether. First of all, it is *truth,* not opinion, preference, or tradition. Second, it is *in love,* not the exclamation just before the door slams. It requires love, tact, kindness, forthrightness, calm, consideration, and willingness to hear the other side. It does not come on like a dive bomber, nor does it dance around the issue. No. It comes to the point without skewering its subject.

How do you do it?

I do not think there is any easy way. Before we wrestle

up the courage to "speak our mind" on a touchy subject, Satan will always frighten us with, "It'll provoke a fight." Or, "She's not ready. You want to get the silent treatment the rest of the week?" Our fear of fights or rejection can prevent this one thing that will rocket a relationship into the heavenly age. But it has to be done. "For God has not given us the spirit of timidity, but of power and love and discipline" (II Timothy 1:7).

When I began trying it with my wife, I tended to blurt the problem out in machine gun fashion. If she wasn't knocked down by the blast, the holes in her psyche kept the blood flowing.

Gradually, though, we have both learned to express things calmly and assuredly. We promise not to blow up at one another. However, if there is anger, we have agreed that before responding, we should be given time to think.

Even little things can be difficult. A friend of mine told me his wife bought him a pair of water skis for his birthday as well as a life vest and tow line. He was apoplectic. "We don't even have a boat!"

"We'll rent one," she replied.

"I can't believe it," he went on. "Where did you get the idea that I wanted water skis?"

"Well, every time we went into the store, you would walk over and look at them. So I bought them for you."

"Good grief! It's a good thing I didn't go over and look at the giant stuffed gorilla!"

She was hurt.

A few days later they were driving in the car. He said, "Can I talk to you about something personal?"

She said sure, anything he wanted.

"Can we take back the skis?"

It's a little funny to an outsider, but we all know what pressure a sensitive issue can bring.

But these are minor issues compared to the problems that can drive a man into oblivion. What about a bad habit she may have? Or a weakness? Or a sin she may commit? No wife is perfect.

Let me offer some thoughts from other Scriptures.

First, ask *is this a wrong that needs to be confronted, or should I cover it?* Peter gives us a powerful word in I Peter 4:8: "Above all, keep fervent in your love for one another, because love covers a multitude of sins."

Any marriage experiences numerous slips of the tongue, wrongs, and mistakes which, if rigorously confronted every time they happen, could lead to hurt on both sides. Many times the answer for a wrong is simply to "cover" it, forgive *and forget* without saying a word.

There are other wrongs, needs, or sins that must be confronted. They eat away at you. You need to communicate or you will detonate.

It is a matter of choice. Can I overlook this wrong? Or do I have to speak up about it? Either way is scriptural. It may just be a matter of what you are willing to forget.

Second, you need *to maintain a "statute of limitations" on anger.* Paul says, "Be angry, and yet do not sin; do not let the sun go down on your anger" (Ephesians 4:26). In other words, if you are angry about something, get it out in the open before you get into bed!

Sometimes we are unwilling to discuss something the same day it happens because the timing is not right, or it is too sensitive—like playing with a live grenade. But, in general, it is not fair or right to sit on a slight or offense for months, then sling it at your mate in the heat of argument. If you are angry about something done or said, speak up. Don't wait until next week, next month, or next year. In our house, we are trying to maintain such a statute of limitations of 48 hours. Either discuss it, or it isn't significant, so "cover" it—and forget it.

On the other hand, there are issues so sensitive that it takes time to discuss. A husband just does not have the courage. He does not want to provoke a fight or hurt his wife.

We have found that it is the cultivation of a truth-speaking relationship that is the answer to this situation. At first, it is difficult to speak your mind on a problem. But just as you might slide your body into cold water gradually, so you should get into the "truthing it in love" gradually. Try some little things. Work them through. Then you will be better able to deal with the more serious issues when they occur.

Third, *give the Spirit time to work.* We have all heard about wives nagging husbands, but what about the reverse? I know that it is not too hard for me to begin acting like the marine lieutenant with white gloves. I can "harp about it" with the best of them.

The principle is: Say it once; then let the Spirit work. She won't forget the issue. If it is something you would like her to do, don't keep pushing and hammering away. That just makes her mad or resentful. Let the Spirit work in her heart.

One evening someone called and made a request that I knew my wife would not want to grant. It was, in fact, a highly tense issue at that time between us because I did not agree with her about that particular request. With the person still on the phone, I talked with Val. She was adamant. "No way." As spiritual head of my home, I did not feel good telling the caller "no." Yet, I knew that vetoing Val's feelings could be too divisive and hurt her. I decided that my wife's needs took precedence over the caller's. Though I expressed my own convictions to Val, I told her I would agree to go along with her desires for the moment. I told the caller it was not a good time to meet the request and concluded the conversation. The caller was angry, but so be it. Then I let it sit.

The next day Val called me and told me she had had a change of heart, felt that she had been harsh about the situation, and wanted to know if I felt she should contact the caller and grant the request. I said fine, and that was it.

I had listened to my own advice. I had given the *Spirit* time to work.

Fourth, *be direct.* It is a real temptation to hint, suggest, imply, allude, insinuate, and even manipulate without ever coming out and *saying it!* How we love to avoid being direct. Being direct means making yourself vulnerable. That is, you are leaving no room for error. You can't patch on an excuse afterward by saying, "Oh, I didn't really mean it." No. You lay all the truth out on the table in technicolor. There is no mistake.

Of course, tact, caution, and compassion all figure in the equation. You do not batter your mate or beat her over the head with the Bible. But at the same time, you refuse to skirt around the issue hoping she will "get the message." She can't read your mind. You must communicate.

This is, indeed, the most difficult aspect of speaking the truth in love. Often I go from one extreme of hoping Val will see the problem without me having to mention it, to the other of being so blunt she feels bludgeoned. Balance is required.

Fifth, *refuse to conceal facts from your wife that may be important to her.* A friend offered me tickets to a special event. It so happened that I knew a woman would also attend who happened to be quite flirtatious and a bit too familiar with me. It is a difficult thing to deal with publicly. My response was to refrain from giving her any signals that she might interpret the wrong way, while at the same time trying to maintain an air of social decorum. Val's feeling was simply that she did not like being around the woman. Nonetheless, I wanted to go to the event. I decided not to tell Val that the woman would be there, perhaps in the next seat.

I kept my silence until we had almost reached our seats, but suddenly I realized a bad situation could arise. At the last minute I said to Val, "Oh, by the way, so and so will probably be here."

Val balked a moment, then proceeded with gritted teeth. It did not turn out badly, but she was angry with me because I had not been "up front" from the start. She said, "You could simply have told me, 'Val, I really want to go to this thing, but so and so will be there. I know she's too familiar and flirtatious, but I won't allow her to get away with it. Will you go?' "

It was a significant lesson. Through rough experiences I have found that speaking the truth usually means all the truth, because sooner or later it *will* come out. If your mate discovers that you withhold sensitive information from her, she will grow not to trust you. You are one. Act like it. Otherwise, you will soon be split in half.

Thus, while speaking the truth in love is difficult, it is not impossible. To parody an old proverb, "A long truth tell always begins with the first speak." Be willing to be vulnerable. Truth and love are two commodities you cannot sell to the devil. He specializes in the opposite.

[1] From *Letters to Karen* by Charles Shedd. Published by Abingdon Press. Used with permission.

—9—

Love Her As Your Own Body

One of Christianity's most difficult concepts to grasp is the concept of the Body of Christ. The church is called "the body of Christ." We are all "members of His body."

Paul spells out the doctrine particularly well in I Corinthians 12. He reminds us that the eye cannot say to the hand, "I don't need you." And the head can't say to the feet, "You're good for nothing." Each part of the body needs the other parts to make up the whole.

What is even more majestic is the fact that these Christians, spread out over the world, are all part of something far greater, an organism which the universe has never seen before. We not only belong to Jesus; we not only are a part of Jesus; but we are organically and spiritually linked so that we *are* His body.

One Flesh

You would think that the symbolism as it is carried out in mariage would be easy to understand. Man and woman become "one flesh." When we are joined in marriage, we become parts of one another. Our "better half" is literal. We are halves of a greater whole.

But often we do not see it that way. Although we lip the words, our hearts don't always embrace it. After all, I do not brave my wife's labor pains. She does not scratch when I itch. When I go the barber, it's not her hair that is cut.

Nonetheless, Scripture makes this much clear: when we join together in marriage and sexual intercourse, we are "one body," one flesh, a single entity (I Corinthians 6:15-16; Matthew 19:5; Ephesians 5:31). This becomes the basis for another of Paul's succinct commands to husbands: "Love your wife as your own body" (Ephesians 5:28).

Dr. D.M. Lloyd-Jones's commentaries on Ephesians have been of great help to me on this issue. On first inspection, he says that Paul's words might strike you as meaning, "Love your wife *like* you love your own body." Sort of a golden rule of marriage. But that is not Paul's thought. He is saying, "Love your wife because she *is* your body, an extension of your own body. Her body literally has become your body."

That is rather different. Loving her *like* I love my own body keeps love at arm's length. I can do that with anyone if I so choose. But loving her *because* she is part of me is unique. There is no one else on earth who holds that position.

No Isolation

For this reason a husband can never think of himself

simply as himself. He is no longer in isolation, a swinging single, able to do what he wants when he wants it. He is part of a bigger whole. He must always be thinking in terms of "my wife and me together" rather than just himself.

I first noted this when, while a bachelor, I visited a friend who had been the first one of my high school buddies to marry. We were reminiscing and talking about marriage when he made this comment. "It's interesting how Renee and I have begun to have the same tastes. When we buy clothing, we think in terms of what we would both look good in together. When we go out to eat, we talk about 'our' favorite spot, not mine or hers. It's a new way of thinking for me."

At the time, I thought the notion was very romantic and said to myself, "Got to find some of that for myself!" Nonetheless, it *is* one of the most important elements and ingredients of true romance. It's "us" now, not "you and me." It's "we," not "I." A husband has to break out of his self-centered consciousness and start thinking of everything in relation to "us" as a couple. How will this business trip affect us, not just *my* business? How will buying this item bring pleasure to both of us, not just me?

How Do I Love My Body?

How will I love my wife because she is part of my body? What actions will I take if I begin loving my wife that way?

There are several ways we can look at this from both negative and positive standpoints. What would I not do to my own body? Dr. Lloyd-Jones touched on three thoughts in his book, *Life in the Spirit*. Let me expand on those areas. [1]

Not abuse it. The first thing that comes to mind is the fact that I do not abuse my body. A sane person would not light a match, then extinguish it against his arm. He would not whip his body for fun. He would not willingly drink strychnine, hammer nails into a foot, or put his body on a hook and invite sharks to dinner.

Yet, multitudes of husbands today abuse their wives physically, emotionally, mentally, spiritually. Dr. Susan Forward, author of the book, *Men Who Hate Women, and the Women Who Love Them,* has gathered an immense following of women who claim their husbands are misogynists—haters of women. Such TV fare as "The Burning Bed" and "Fatal Vision" have dramatized this epidemic of malice and abuse. A tidal wave of anger has unleashed itself in homes worldwide.

Clarence W. Hall, in *Adventures for God,* speaks of a Sir Henry Holland, missionary doctor. One of the doctor's strangest duties was replacing women's noses. The local tribesmen were extremely jealous, and one of their traditions allowed a husband to chop off his wife's nose on the slightest suspicion of adultery. If he later discovered her innocence, he often brought her to the doctor to make repairs. One tribesman, though, when told the operation would cost 60 shillings, hesitated. The doctor asked, "Is it not worth the money to have a wife with a nose?" The tribesman replied, "That's a hard question, Doctor Sahib. You see, for 75 shillings I can buy a new wife!"

The cry is different in our age. "For a little litigation, I can divorce my wife and get another!" But it is still the same sort of abuse.

The answer is for a man to allow himself to be controlled by the Spirit, not the emotion of the moment. If he has a tendency toward violence, he should get help in learning to control it and cherish "his" body, his wife.

Not neglect it. The second thing we normally will not do with our bodies is neglect them. We eat. We sleep. We meet the basic needs. Although there are times when we overlook certain functions, our basic attitude is one of sustenance, care, watchfulness.

Similarly, because our wives are our own bodies, we will not neglect them. We will spend time with them, meet their needs, make their happiness our priority. Abraham Lincoln once wrote, "Whatever woman may cast her lot with mine, should any ever do so, it is my intention to do all in my power to make her happy and contented; and there is nothing I can imagine that would make me more unhappy than to fail in the effort."

An artist, while painting the portrait of William Jennings Bryan asked why he wore his hair over his ears. Bryan explained, "There is a romance connected with that. When I began courting Mrs. Bryan, she objected to the way my ears stood out. So to please her, I let my hair grow to cover them."

"But that was many years ago," the artist said. "Why don't you have your hair cut now?"

"Because," Bryan said with a wink, "the romance is still going on."

One who loves his wife *as* his own body will not neglect her. He will find out what her needs are and strive to meet them with all his might.

Not take her for granted. The third negative Dr. Lloyd-Jones mentions is that such a husband will not take his wife for granted.

One bachelor approached a young miss this way as he worked his way up to the great question. "There are quite a lot of advantages in being a bachelor, but there comes a time when one longs for the companionship of another being—a being who will regard one as perfect, as an idol; whom one can treat as one's absolute property; who will be kind and faithful when times are hard; who will share one's joys and sorrows—"

As he spoke, he noted a sympathetic glow in her eyes, and she nodded in agreement. But then she jarred him by saying, "So you're thinking of buying a dog? I think it's a fine idea. Do let me help you choose one."

We may smile, yet those sentiments are exactly what many men express in their marriages. They want someone who will regard them as "perfect, an idol;" someone who is "their absolute property." That kind of attitude breeds the curse of complacency. You begin to take such a woman for granted. You lose respect for her.

I find that it takes conscious, continual effort and work to avoid this pitfall. It is too easy to come home, sink onto the sofa, and not move again until dinner or bedtime. It is too easy to loll in front of the television rather than make genuine conversation. It is too easy in the rush and crush of our careening world to forget the flowers, the cards, the little notes, the sweet nothings in the ear, and the long embraces in the dark—not for passion, just for romance. It's too easy to simply huff and puff along while your house is blowing down.

Erma Bombeck was asked what personal possession gave her the most value for the money. She replied, "I would have to say my wedding ring. For years, it has done its job. It has led me not into temptation. It has reminded my husband numerous times at parties that it's time to go home. It has been a source of relief to a dinner companion. It has been a status symbol in the maternity ward. It has reminded me every day of the last 30 years that I have someone who loves me."

Husbands, take a look at your wedding ring. Is that what you see?

Loving Positively

Yet, loving your wife as your own body is not just avoiding the potholes of abuse, neglect, and taking her for granted. It is much more. What is the positive side? Perhaps framing several pointed questions would help. Ask . . .

What nourishes her? Paul says the husband is to "nourish" his wife. The word means to "give what is needed to sustain life." The root idea is to nurture, bring up, or rear, as in the case of children. But I am certain Paul has no intention of suggesting that a husband "parent" his wife. Incidentally, many husbands do precisely that, treating their wives as children. It is, however, lethal to intimacy and warmth. Rather, what Paul is saying is that the husband must provide the nourishment she needs to remain healthy. That calls for both physical, spiritual, and psychological food.

Take the physical, for instance. Most husbands who read this book are probably able providers. Their wives are not roaming the streets begging for bread. Yet, there can be an under-riding and sinister attitude in this. A husband can act as though he resents every penny he gives her. He can take her out to eat, but at the same time display an air of bitterness that she wants dessert. "What do you think I am? Made of money?" he replies. He can grill her about how she spends the money for food as though she were an idiot without any idea of how to cut corners and save. He can grumble when she splurges on shrimp for a special meal. Or complain when she decides on a night off and asks him to pay for the pizza.

Or take clothing. Do you complain, saying she "has a

whole closet of clothes so why does she need a new dress?" Or do you resent it that the beautician costs so much and gripe about the money, all the while saying little or nothing about her beauty or that she takes care of her looks—for you? The nurturing, nourishing husband will see that his wife is built up along these lines.

An important test occurs when a wife is ill. How does the husband react then? With anger and resentment because of an inconvenience or cost? With impatience when she needs to stay in bed? With exasperation because she may ask you to stay home from work to watch the kids? Should the kids, especially younger ones, always be her responsibility—even when she is sick? Should a business consider an employee's wife's illness reason for him to stay home when there are young children and no babysitter?

One afternoon my wife called the office. "Mark, I'm throwing up, my stomach is turning inside out, and Nicole is playing demolition derby on the first floor. Can you come home a little early?"

For once I didn't hedge. I said I would do my best to get home promptly. I just had to clear it with the boss. My boss was most understanding, and I sped home.

Sure enough, my wife was in terrible shape. Worse, Nicole had sprinkled the contents of the pantry all over the living room floor. My first evil thought was, "Val asked me to come home so she wouldn't have to deal with this." My second wretched thought was, "She better not get sick like this again." And then the first twinge of real character hit. "Is this the way you should think about or treat your wife who normally has the house in perfect shape every day? Is your attitude one of real compassion?"

I was guilty. Immediately I repented, began to whistle as I worked, and even thanked the Lord for Nicole's inadvertent spilling of the beans by the ledge to the cellar so they could be swept up easily! It was a real change of heart for me.

That kind of change is critical to marital health. If a husband feels resentment about his wife's sicknesses, money needs, or other physical concerns, he will decimate the relationship.

Now consider the psychological. Examine yourself and think about what you discussed with her the last few nights. Anything of substance? Anything about "us"? Any special thoughts or feelings? Or was it mostly, "Pass the salt," and "Did you take the dog out?" A woman can feel psychologically mutilated by the strong silent type who is a bit weak in the mind and tongue.

Cliff Barrows often speaks of the twelve words that hold a marriage together. "I am wrong." "I am sorry." "Please forgive me." And, "I love you."

A man does not have to be comedian of the year or orator of the decade to express a few good words each evening. I find it helpful actually to prepare my conversation for the evening. On the way home from work I will often muse about some subject we might discuss in depth. That is emotional nourishment.

That's not to say I am a whiz at this. I have had my silent times. But you can work at it.

Still, be careful. You can deluge a woman, too. There is a story about Bernard Shaw in which a reporter visited him and his wife. As Shaw and the reporter talked, the philosopher's wife sat there calmly knitting. Suddenly, the reporter turned to Mrs. Shaw. "You seem most absorbed in your knitting," he said. "Is it a strong interest?" "Not really," answered Mrs. Shaw. "But you see, I've heard these stories of Bernard's for years now, and if I didn't do something with my hands, I'd strangle him."

A wife needs space, too.

Then there is also the spiritual. What can you do to nourish your wife spiritually? We have talked about that in the chapter on "Sanctify Her." But I also find that sharing an insight or experience from the day helps. Of course, there is Bible study, prayer, and church activities, but a wife likes to feel she has a spiritual leader in the house, not just a salesman for someone else's product.

An interesting statement from Paul is found in I Corinthians 7:1-5. Paul writes,

> *Now concerning the things about which you wrote, it is good for a man not to touch a woman. But because of immoralities, let each man have his own wife, and let each woman have her own husband. Let the husband fulfill his duty to his wife, and likewise also the wife to her husband. The wife does not have authority over her own body, but the husband does; and likewise also the husband does not have authority over his own body, but the wife does. Stop depriving one another, except by agreement for a time that you may devote yourselves to prayer, and come together again lest Satan tempt you because of your lack of self-control.*

On first inspection, one is tempted to think this simply refers to a mutual meeting of each other's sexual needs. But notice Paul says, "Let the husband fulfill his *duty* to his wife." What is his duty? To meet her needs, just as she is to meet his. The problem, though, is that many husbands think a wife's sexual needs are similar to his own.

But they are not. Studies have shown that men and women are very different when it comes to sexual needs. While a man may seek primarily a climax and a release of inner sexual tension, a woman looks at it from an entirely different perspective. Her sexual needs center more in personal demonstrations of affection—through touch, compliments, embraces, supportiveness, and encouragement—rather than simply an hour of high sexual excitement.

I began to realize this when one wife said to me, "When my husband starts to play kiss and hug, I can tell what he really wants because it's the only time he shows me any affection."

I noted that and took a look at my own life. Sure enough, I discovered my own transgressions. Too often I was affectionate only when I wanted something more. Val and I began discussing our different needs in that area—very openly and forthrightly. It was not easy at first, but gradually we let everything out. It has enhanced not only our sexual life, but every other aspect of our lives. Now I am more aware of her desires and she of mine. Communication of those things is essential. If you as the husband are not sure what your wife needs and wants, ask her. Keep asking her. Take inventory every now and then. "How am I meeting your needs, Hon? Do I get an A, B, C, D, or E? What am I missing? Where am I falling short?" The test of a good marriage is each partner's ability to be truthful and open. If one is too threatened to be direct, something is wrong. Start talking at that level and work together to define your needs and responsibilities to each other in this area. As you seek to understand what gives the other pleasure, you will find your personal relationship growing closer and the physical relationship more enjoyable.

Do you cherish her? Again, Paul makes the statement that a man "cherishes" his body. The term translated "cherish" means to "keep warm, foster with tender care."

It was used in secular literature of a mother bird sitting on her eggs, warming and protecting them. Paul uses the word in I Thessalonians 2:7 where he says, "We proved to be gentle among you, as a nursing mother tenderly cares for her own children." The words, "tenderly care," capture the scene. You can see the new mother gazing down upon her newborn as she cradles it, her eyes glowing with tenderness, sympathy, and love. No one could wrestle this baby out of her arms. No person could attack or molest the baby without going through her first.

In the same way, God expects that a husband will exhibit such tender care and protection toward his wife.

I witnessed a husband doing this once when a church member spoke harshly with his wife. Although his wife said nothing, he stepped up to the man, saying, "I ask that you show respect to my wife. You may be angry with her, but you have no right to show disrespect."

Wives need to know their husbands will protect them.

The one who has the greatest impact on a woman's life will be her husband. What he says, how he says it, how he speaks of her in public and elsewhere will either boost or buffet her.

A wife confided to me that her esteem had fallen in the last few years. I asked her why. "My husband just puts me down so much." I attended a dinner at their house. I was astounded at the numerous subtle ways her husband criticized her, amply exposing the reasons for her lack of esteem.

- When she told a story, he corrected her several times, pointing out inaccuracies in her "facts."
- When she spoke, he would interrupt with his own version of the story, or else start in on his own.

• No comments were made by him about the fine dinner she had prepared, even though everyone else was most complimentary.

• When a newsworthy item was discussed, her opinion was described several times as "foolish" and "stupid."

• When she tripped and spilled something, his face clouded, and he made a sarcastic joke about her clumsiness.

This kind of attitude destroys self-esteem and a relationship. There is no protection, no care, no cherishing.

On the other hand, one husband chose to demonstrate to the world his feelings toward his wife. He placed the following advertisement in the classified section of a respected city newspaper.

> *I am responsible for all debts and obligations of my wife, Selma, both present and future, and am delighted to be the provider for a woman who has borne me two fine children, listened patiently to all my gripes, and with an overabundance of love and care made the past fifteen years of my life the happiest I have known. On this, our fifteenth wedding anniversary, I am proud to express my gratitude publicly.*

Now there is a man who cherishes his wife in the biblical sense.

What makes your wife feel cherished? What gives her self-respect and a sense of personal value? If you don't know, ask her. And begin applying the principles that will meet those needs.

Are you participating in her development as a person? A body needs exercise. Spiritual and mental muscles must develop tone. Psychological nerves need tending. Your body must realize its full potential. Even so, a husband must give of his energy and time to develop his wife as a person, as a woman, as a lover.

Every now and then I read about a grandmother who, at age 67 or 72, just graduated from college. Occasionally the newspapers print a report about some female mover and shaker who has gotten the government in an uproar about an injustice. Husbands need to encourage their wives to get involved, to stretch themselves, to try something new, to take risks. A man who demands that his wife wait on him hand and foot will quickly transform her from a self-respecting lover to a self-denigrating woman with no achievements of her own. The king of the house will lose the power behind the throne.

Our world cries out today for volunteers. Organizations that once thrived because godly women gave of their time and lifeblood joyfully, now suffer because many of the women are working. But most women who do not need to be in the workplace could find greater fulfillment and personhood in serving God in volunteer areas. Husbands who encourage this kind of spiritual and personal development will see their wives flower and bloom.

Also critical in this matter is praying together. Are you praying for one another's growth? Do you do so together, and alone?

Homemade, a take-home bulletin insert, featured this quote in the April 1979 edition: "Over the past fifteen years, sociology professor Dr. Elaine Walster has studied the differences between "passionate" and "compassionate" love, and interviewed or observed more than 100,000 persons. She found that, for most couples, intense passion lasts six months to two and a half years. Clearly, for love to persist, it has to move beyond that first romantic frenzy into the warm intensity of deep friendship."

What Dr. Walster saw was the need to become friends and do as friends do. Kenneth Chafin, in his book, *Is There A Family in the House?* asks the question, "What nurtures a relationship, feeds it, and makes it stronger?" He offers six suggestions, but the list could be endless. "(1) The things you do together as a couple. (2) The problems you work on together. (3) Being with other friends together. (4) Deciding who your friends will be and the activities you will be involved in together. (5) Discovering how much privacy each of you needs and learning to honor it. (6) Involving yourself in some ministry to others together." [2]

Charlie Shedd adds some more in his book, *Letters To Philip.* "(1) We will aim to be 'best friends.' (2) At least once a week we will go out together. (3) We make it a goal to be honest all the way. (4) As an ideal, forty-eight hours will be our hiding limit. (5) We will aim for total mercy and forgiveness. (6) We will respect each other's privacy. (7) We will remember that mystery is a blessing." [3]

These are the kinds of things that encourage the development of a relationship and of the persons within that relationship.

Sometimes the Lord has to wake us men up. But He will do it. Somehow.

[1] Our appreciation to Baker Book House for use of material from *Life in the Spirit* by D. Martin Lloyd-Jones. Copyrighted 1973. Used with permission.

[2] Reprinted by permission from *Is There a Family in the House?* by Kenneth Chafin, Word Books.

[3] From *Letters to Philip* by Charles Shedd © 1968, Doubleday and Co., Inc. Used with permission.

—10—
Do You Hear What She's Saying?

I was sure I had the snappy and certain solution to my wife's problem. Rapidly I spelled out the details. But Val only zoomed into further frustration. Finally, she blurted, "Can't I just express my feelings without you going off on a speech?"

At first, such a response amazed me. But as my marriage grows and I learn more about husbands relating to wives and vice versa, I am astonished at how hard it is to *hear* what a wife is saying. When it comes to problems, feelings, and circumstances, men often look at things very differently from women.

You show me a broken wagon, and I can give you four steps to fixing the thing. Show my wife a broken wagon and she wants to take the child's hand, sit down, and say, "I bet you're upset. Tell me about it."

Or, perhaps someone at church or home is getting on your nerves. My reaction is to consider how to get back on the right wavelength. But a wife might not be interested, initially, in finding a solution. Her response might be, "It's not right for them to treat me like that. Don't you agree?" Most often, she wants her husband to listen, not analyze. Certainly not disagree or offer logic.

It is a hard lesson for many of us. Others may swagger in, hear their wife's pained remarks about something, and then proceed to tell her how to realign the universe. But often, sitting down together on the couch, good eye contact, and a kiss and hug are what she wants. And needs.

Frankly, it still amazes me. A wife wants a little kindness. Men want action. She longs for a listening ear. We hear three words, and we're ready to haul it into the shop and tinker with it. She seeks understanding, tenderness, intimacy. Our response is, "Let's not get all lovey-dovey about this. Let's fix the thing."

Men and women regard communication differently. It is part of the way God made us. If we were exactly alike, one of us would not be necessary. But it can create conflict. That's why this chapter is entitled, "Do you hear what she's saying?" Many husbands hear their wives' words, but not their undercurrents.

One man I know maintains that few people today listen at all. To prove his point, he shook hands with the hostess at a party and said, "I'm sorry I'm late, but it took me longer to strangle my aunt than I expected." The hostess simply beamed back at him, saying, "Yes, indeed, I'm so happy you made it anyway."

Talk is important to a woman. Talk builds intimacy even more than sex, travel, a beautiful home, going to restaurants, diamonds—anything else you can name. She wants to feel that she knows her man through and through. More importantly, she wants to know what he thinks about her. Some men go for months, even years, without an intimate word. I read of one man who ended up in a counseling room because his wife was in deep emotional pain. She was convinced he no longer loved her. The counselor finally asked him, "Sir, when was the last time you told your wife you loved her?" He replied, "When I married her 25 years ago I told her I loved her and if it ever changed I'd let her know." Apparently, it hadn't changed. But she didn't know it.

One night my wife and I were watching television. She had expressed a need to "talk more" and suddenly I had an idea. I suggested, "How about a quick Bible study?" She wasn't feeling up to it at the moment; I was upset. I said, "Well, you wanted me to talk more, and now here's a chance. But you don't want to do it." She replied, "If we study some verses, we'll just talk about the Bible." I went on, "But we're sitting here watching television. We're not talking at all. If we study a passage, at least we'll be talking to one another." She replied, "But we wouldn't be talking about us."

Bells rang in my head. *So that's it,* I thought. It's not just talking that is important. It is talking about "us."

That was a hammerblow of awakening. I had never thought about that before. There is a difference between talking about what happened at work, what happened at home, who called, or even a Bible study—and talking about "us." My reaction is often, "But I know everything about you from before we were married. And you know everything about me from the moment I was born! Since then we've been through it all together. So what's there to discuss?"

"Us."

What about us?

Our dreams (together—not just mine or hers, but ours).

Our hopes. And especially, how much she means to me. She wants to know how I feel about her cooking, her mothering, her looks. Husbands need to encourage their wives consistently, appropriately, and honestly.

Think about it. What do you want to hear when you have fixed the oven, brought home a rose, or taken her to dinner? What about your looks? Your physique? Have you ever wanted her to tell you, "You have the greatest muscles"?

On paper it sounds a bit foolish. But we all need that reinforcement, that encouragement, that certainty that we matter to someone.

Take another situation. What happened when you last had a disagreement? Did you get mad and sling some hot words at her? Did she retaliate and bring up an old oversight on your part?

I have found that partners often expect one another to read the other's mind. The husband is supposed to know what she is upset about and vice versa.

That's a little hard to take. So we retort, "What am I supposed to do? Get inside your head?"

Have you been there? A marital relationship has so many different levels of communication and subtle innuendoes that you are likely to miss them if you are not watching closely. Both wives and husbands need to hear what the other is saying. But how?

Let's look at several principles from Scripture on the issue of listening.

Quick to Hear

First, James tells us to be "quick to hear, slow to speak and slow to anger" (James 1:19).

Notice the portrait: *quick* to hear; *slow* to speak; *slow* to anger. The person has his head cocked, his full attention riveted on the speaker. He is struggling to absorb every word. His mental computer busily sifts the other information pouring in through his senses.

He does not speak until he has listened completely, thoroughly. In fact, what he does say may mirror back to his wife what she has said. He wants to understand her, to make sure he has gotten the message.

When you are quick to hear and slow to speak, you are like Job's counselors, who, for all their faults, still did not say a word for seven days after they saw how great his pain was.

There are also a number of phrases such a person avoids completely. Like . . .

"Didn't I tell you that would happen?"

"Won't you ever learn?"

"Now why on earth did you do that?"

"If I've told you once, I've told you a hundred times."

"I can't believe you actually feel that way."

"This is dumb. Really, really dumb."

"You shouldn't feel that way."

"Nobody on earth ever handled it like that!"

"Look, I'm sorry already. Will you get off my back?"

"I'M TELLING YOU, I AM NOT ANGRY!"

"I'm warning you to lay off. *Now!*"

The quick to hear, slow to speak attitude is an attitude Jesus displayed in Scripture. Even when He rebuked the Pharisees, He usually listened to them first. In the case of the sinful woman in Luke 7, He was patient with Simon the Pharisee, examining him to discover the proper response.

When it comes to anger, a good reminder is: "Never yell at one another unless the house is on fire or the ship is sinking!" Scripture says it another way. "A man's discretion makes him slow to anger, and it is his glory to overlook a transgression" (Proverbs 19:11).

Yet, as A.P. Herbert says, "The conception of two people living together for twenty-five years without having a cross word suggests a lack of spirit only admired in sheep." There are times when anger is appropriate. But the key verse there is, "Be angry, and yet do not sin; do not let the sun go down on anger" (Ephesians 4:26). You can be angry. Just don't resort to sinful methods, words, attitudes, or actions. And do not let it build up between you.

Why are we to be this way? Because, "the anger of man does not achieve the righteousness of God" (James 1:20). No matter how certain you are of being right, you have to take a look at God Himself. How long has He been tolerating cheats, liars, adulterers, murderers, thieves, and revilers? Centuries. His righteousness means that He will always do the right thing regardless of what anyone else does.

My greatest problem in this area is stopping and thinking before I respond. If I can just tell myself, "Now look, Mark, think. Think! *Think!* Before you speak. She's upset. Give her time to talk."

Our tendency is to push when someone shoves. But we have to learn to lean back a little.

Weep With Those Who Weep

Second, Romans 12:15 commands, "Rejoice with those who rejoice, and weep with those who weep." Many Christians tend to forget feelings—partly because they are so sure they have the truth, and partly because the human response is to want to solve the problem, not tarry in it. But often a wife needs a man who tenderly reassures her of his support and love, not a guy who fires a divine line at her like a rock from a slingshot. Sitting down, listening, and telling her you understand—or at least are trying to—is what she often needs.

When Jesus stood outside Lazarus's tomb, He wept. Unabashedly. Everyone could see the depth of His love. He was moved.

Sometimes a wife simply wants to know that her man is moved with her. She does not want to be alone.

An important consideration is that a husband might understand her feelings, but may not feel that same emotion at the moment. Does this invalidate his understanding?

There is one important way this can be balanced in a marriage: By the husband beginning to show genuine concern about his wife's state of heart. He should never respond, "Why do you feel that way? I wouldn't feel that way." Or, "You shouldn't get all upset about this little thing." If she feels it, that's enough. Her feelings are valid, however unimportant they may appear compared to the problem of nuclear holocaust or world hunger.

Furthermore, a man should not be ashamed of tears. Warmth, compassion, concern, care, and touch are not forbidden in the masculine vocabulary. He who is most masculine of all wept, showed compassion, touched, sympathized. The Lord holds such a high premium on tears that Scripture says He has stored them in a bottle and recorded them in His book (Psalm 56:8).

A man who can take his wife's hands in his—however rough, calloused, and brown—draw her heart to his and weep, is one who will never find his wife cold in his embrace for other things.

Give Grace

A third principle for listeners comes from Ephesians 4:29. "Let no unwholesome word proceed from your mouth, but only such a word as is good for edification according to the need of the moment, that it may give grace to those who hear."

To live out this verse requires the greatest of listening skills. One must hear with all his heart and soul to spot that "word good for edification" to fill the "need of the moment" that he might "give grace." David Augsburger graphically illustrates that kind of listening in his book, *The Freedom of Forgiveness.* He says, "To listen is the queen of compliments; to ignore, the chief of insults. To become human everyone needs listeners and to be human he too must learn to listen.

"Do you know how to listen? Or do your eyes stray and betray your wandering interests? (A good listener listens with his eyes too, you know).

"Do you let others' words and ideas fly by while you plan your next comment, cooking up some sage word with which to stun them at the first opportunity?

"Do you interrupt others, or even worse, second-guess them, trying to finish the line for a friend, or coach him when he stumbles for a word?

"Do you probe, question, interrogate, cross-examine, thus suggesting impatience or superiority?

"Or can you truly listen? Can you go beyond merely hearing words and phrases to catch ideas? And beyond ideas, to the feelings? Beyond the questions to the true intent?

"That's listening—with love for others.

"Love is a warm listener." [1]

Do you express that warmth to your wife? Do you search for the right word, the word that edifies, builds up?

Mark Twain used to say, "The difference between the right word and the almost right word is the difference between lightning and the lightning bug." Do you struggle to discern the need of the moment? Are you concerned about giving grace?

Notice Paul's thought here.

First, we are to let "no unwholesome word" proceed from our mouths. The "unwholesome" word is the "putrid, foul, revolting" word. A curse. A slam. A put-down. A sarcastic gibe. A harsh brush-off. The listener listens to himself as well as to others. What is coming out of your mouth? Slime, grime, or the sublime? Dirt or loam? A crushing blow or a caring boost?

Second, we grope for the word that "is good for edification," the clause that builds up. This requires the deftest ear and eye. The true listener grasps this because he sees beneath the surface. He knows what makes his wife's face light up and her spirit sing. Ask yourself, "What builds my wife up?" "What touches her down deep?" Is it an "I love you," a compliment, a hug, a card with tender words inscribed, or a kind letter?

Third, we strive to discern the "need of the moment." Every moment has its particular "need," its cry in the night. Sometimes the need is for a backrub. Other times it is a kiss or a hug. Other times it is a long listen on the couch, or a tender word, or some encouragement. The listening husband seeks to perceive that need, and then meet it.

Fourth, learn to "give grace." Giving grace is supplying supernatural power to overcome the problem of the moment. We can't do that. Only God can. But we can be channels. We can be the spark that sets the fuse on fire.

What gives grace? Ask yourself, "What are the things

that have stuck with me all my life? What words have transformed me?" Those are the kinds of words that give grace. It takes an expert listener to catch them. But they are there.

Recently, I gave my wife a special card for no reason other than to encourage her. I have given her lots of cards, but she said to me, "That was the best card you ever gave me." When I asked her why, she said it was because of what I'd written inside. I've gone over that card now several times, looking for the hidden words that turned her switch. But you can't just repeat yourself. Locate the principle and employ it frequently.

Listen For Your Life

Men who listen to their wives with these principles in mind will never lack an audience or a respect-filled spouse. And some time, your very life may depend on your ability to listen at the right moment.

A poignant article by Leon Jones appeared in *Christian Herald,* June 1987, that illustrates this well.

Leon Jones had gotten into the habit of not listening to anyone in his family. One night his six-year-old daughter came downstairs complaining of a light going off and on in her room. Leon told her to go to bed and not disturb him any more. He was engrossed in a baseball game.

A little later his wife noticed that the lights in the house flickered. "Honey, did you see that?"

Leon brushed her off and went back to his game. Finally, though, he noticed it, too. He went to the stairway. Toxic fumes stung his nostrils. He ran up the stairs and flung open the nursery door. Smoke billowed out. Everyone began yelling "Fire!" while Leon dropped to the floor trying to see through the smoke. A fan had shorted out, and lay smoldering on the rug.

But his concern wasn't the fan at the moment. It was the baby, Greg. He couldn't find him.

He reached the crib. Nothing.

He rubbed his eyes and got another breath. Suddenly, through the smoke, he spotted the baby curled up in a corner of the crib, frightened and trembling. He reached out and pulled the baby toward him, then grabbed him and ran for the door. Moments later, the fan burst into flames. When they reached the street, they heard the fire sirens screaming in the distance.

In a motel later that night, as his family slept, Leon thought about what had happened. Suddenly, he began to realize how he had taken his family for granted all those years, and also how much he loved them. He prayed, and determined to really listen to his family, to express his feelings, and to love them like he had never loved them before.

For many of us, it takes a real jolt to get us out of our self-centered stupors and into what's important. For Leon Jones, it was a fire. For Pat Williams in *Rekindled,* it was his wife's emotional collapse.

What will it take for you?

[1] From *Freedom of Forgiveness* by David Augsburger. Copyright 1970. Moody Bible Institute of Chicago. Moody Press. Used by permission.

—11—

Do not Be Embittered Against Her!

"If thine enemy wrong thee, buy each of his children a drum." So says an old Chinese proverb. I remember why my brother bought his first drum set: to play in a band. But my parents were convinced this was the revenge of the Banshee.

Getting revenge seems to be ingrained in us. People, Christians included, find remarkable means of getting even with those who hurt, offend, and cross them. In particular, husbands and wives are known to become embroiled in push, slash, and mash battles that last decades.

But revenge is neither cute, good-natured, or insane. It is often carefully conceived and plotted. Even if it is not carried out, just thinking about what you would like to do can be a grim pleasure. I even read about one couple, who, in lieu of divorce, decided to maintain a forced separation. The husband went outside, pulled the cord on his chainsaw, and proceeded to cut the house in half, presumably to clearly divide his half from hers.

Paul Saw the Sinister Edge

Paul must have meditated long and hard about such scenarios because he mentions the problem in Colossians 3:19. "Husbands, love your wives, and do not be embittered against them." In other passages, he tells us to love them like Christ loved the church, love them as our own bodies, nourish them and cherish them. But here he makes a real leap. "And do not be embittered against them." How did that idea creep in?

The Greek word means to "embitter, exasperate, cause to become angry." Husbands can become embittered toward their wives with amazing ease. I visited a married college buddy one day. When I pulled up in the car, I caught him stalking up the sidewalk. His lips were bunched into a bulldog pout. His eyes were aflame. He was pounding his fist into his thigh. I said in a friendly tone, "Hey Kent, what's going on?"

He flinched when he saw me and smiled, then his face clouded. "If *she* says one more thing I'm going to . . . "

I waited for the pronouncement. But suddenly his wife's voice swept down from the window. "Kent! Oh, Kent!"

Kent sucked in a deep breath, then turned to me. "Think long and hard before you get married, bud! Take it from me."

Fortunately, Kent and his wife saw better days after that. But many marriages end up in a dumpster—each dumps the other. Why is this?

Reasons For Embitterment

Undoubtedly there are as many reasons to become embittered as there are husbands. When I first conceived this chapter, I instantly thought of a number of behaviors that could make a man bitter. They were things a wife might do like being domineering, manipulative, rejecting, overly jealous, critical, malicious.

But as I looked more closely at the issue, I realized that a husband's bitterness is *his* response to his circumstances. The circumstances do not cause his bitterness. The way he chooses to respond does. Thus, I am convinced that no husband typically becomes embittered because his wife happens to be domineering or anything else. Rather, it is because he is dealing with his situation unscripturally and sinfully. No husband can excuse his wrong feelings, resentment, anger, and bitterness by saying, "My wife made me do it." No, he is responsible for his own feelings.

So as we proceed in this section, let's look particularly at the responses and wrong actions a *husband* can take that lead to embitterment, not his wife's behavior.

First, a husband can become bitter toward his wife because he does not understand the differences between men and women. If a man goes into marriage thinking his wife will soon be his best football, fishing, and hunting buddy, he will probably be disappointed. Even though she may have gone along with such things *before* marriage, she may now begin saying "no." She may even admit that she went along earlier because she wanted to be with him and liked him. But, in reality, it was him she wanted, not the activity.

A husband needs to spend time seeking to understand the basic differences outlined in chapter four. Books by Dr. James Dobson, Dr. Charles Swindoll, and others provide this kind of insight as well. Often I have heard husbands complain about their wives' "foibles" or "negative traits" when the real need is for him to understand those basic differences between men and women.

Second, a husband can become bitter because of inappropriate responses to his wife's behavior. A wife may make mistakes, or even have weaknesses that become real irritations. But the problem is not her. It is his resonse to her. What are some inappropriate responses?

Trying to force her into his way of doing things. As chapter three explained, the curse threw all of us into a feminist/chauvinist mindset. The wife may seek to dominate her husband, either subtly or openly. The husband may try to crush his wife by forcing on her whatever expectations and ideas he may have about marriage and their life together.

For instance, she learns that one of his favorite meals from childhood is pot roast. So she surprises him with one. But her idea of pot roast is vastly different from his. He takes one taste and says, "What's this? This isn't like my Mom used to make it!" Those are fighting words in any marriage.

One man commented to me, "I can't believe the way my wife was cleaning out the closet last weekend. It took her hours. I could have had that thing straightened up in 15 minutes." He told me they often have sharp disputes about how the dishes should be done, how the house should be cleaned, and so forth. But it was *his* problem. He was not willing to let his wife be herself, to do things her way.

A husband can easily fall into a bitter struggle with his wife when he begins trying to foist on her all his ideas about how everything should be done. He needs to let her exercise her own sovereignty in those areas in which she has authority and/or skills.

Dishonesty about his feelings. Have you ever been engaged in this scenario? The husband seems a little touchy and irritable, so the wife asks, "Is something wrong?" Actually there is. He's a bit angry about some things that have happened. But he won't admit his feelings for several reasons. For one, he is afraid the issue may be too sensitive, and it will provoke a disagreement. For another, he does not want to hurt her feelings. And for a third, he is not used to "telling all."

So what happens is that he tells her nothing is wrong, or else he brings up something else, not the real issue, and discusses that as though it was the issue. Although brushed aside, the problem eats away at him, and his resentment grows.

Such husbands have to learn to "speak the truth in love," as chapter ten discussed. He cannot hide his thoughts for long. They will come out one way or another, and if not in an honest, loving sharing of truth, it will be in bitterness and anger.

Failure to forgive. The root of bitterness is the failure to forgive. She did something, even way back when. She may not even have known she hurt him. He never brought it up. He thought he would just overlook it. But somehow he can't. He keeps thinking about it, and the wound festers.

There are only two ways, scripturally, to respond to a hurt: cover it (forgive and *forget*) or confront it. Denial, repression, and anger are not appropriate responses.

Non-acceptance. In any relationship, one is bound to discover weaknesses, idiosyncrasies, and foibles that can be endearing sometimes, and irksome at other times. One of the most basic elements in the area of self-acceptance concerns one's own drawbacks: If it is something you can change, change it. If you can't, thank God and accept it as a gift from Him that makes you unique.

The same principle applies to marital acceptance. Certain things about your wife may be unchangeable. They are part of the package. You must accept them. Even more, you may need to go far beyond that and choose to make that quality a reason for greater love and compassion. I remember Charles Swindoll speaking at a chapel program I attended. He referred to a friend of his who had a large, splotchy birthmark on his face. Since that friend never showed any embarrassment or constraint about his condition, Dr. Swindoll asked him about it. The friend replied that when he was young, his father told him that that birthmark was where the angel kissed him, and it was God's way of marking him as His child. The friend said, "I got so that I felt bad for anyone who *didn't* have a birthmark like mine!"

Imagine if all husbands regarded those unchangeable things about their wives as marks of special love and identification! Irritation would give way to intimacy and unity.

Comparing. Some husbands find it easy to point out to their wives all the ways they ought to be like so-and-so. But comparisons are unfair to everyone concerned. It is the ultimate rejection. What you are saying is that the other woman is better than your wife, and you prefer her.

If a husband has an honest complaint, it should never be expressed in the phraseology of comparison. "Why don't you keep house like Mary? Now she really knows how to make things comfortable." He needs to convey his feelings in a positive, encouraging way. "I appreciate it when you have the house looking good when I get home. It makes me feel more comfortable."

Not knowing how to disagree amicably. Undoubtedly, the primary way a husband develops bitterness is through improper disagreement techniques. One of the best books I have ever read on the issue is called *Caring Is Not Enough,* by David Augsburger. In it the author discusses the issue of fair fighting and outlines thirty wrong ways to wage marital "war." For each of those wrong responses, he provides an appropriate biblical answer. Any husband who finds himself repeatedly embroiled in marital conflicts probably has not learned how to work through disagreements properly. I would recommend a study of this book.

But, there are times when a husband and wife need to disagree agreeably. I believe fervently in Paul's dictum, "being of the same mind, maintaining the same love, united in spirit, intent on one purpose" (Philippians 2:2). There may be times in marriage when a husband has to make a decision with which the wife does not agree. However, I have found that, more often than not, those can be bad decisions. Paul encourages Christians to be "of the same mind." That means working toward real agreement.

I was astounded when I learned that the board of some 80 elders and pastors at Grace Community Church in California does not make *any* decision without complete agreement on the part of everyone. If there are points of dissent, the different forces present "position papers" in order to work through the issue. Their goal is to reach *real* unity on the issue on the basis of what the Bible says and how the Holy Spirit is leading. Dr. John MacArthur told me that this process has led his church of over 7,000 to make such major decisions only when there is real agreement. From the evidence exhibited by the ministry of Grace Community Church, his idea is a sound one.

But if this is true of 80 leaders in a church, how much more true ought it to be between a husband and wife? My suspicion is that a husband who does not seek to reach mutual agreement with his wife is either being impatient, unwilling to wait on God, or inconsiderate. In fact, he may be expressing chauvinism rather than Christianity. In addition, his actions may reveal a deeper problem than the one apparent at that moment.

Impatience. The little catch slogan, PBPGINFWMY—"Please be patient, God is not finished with me yet!"—applies to wives and husbands as well as friends, family members, and strangers.

The thing that helps me in this area is to step outside of myself and examine how I like to be treated. For instance, when I am driving on a crowded highway and someone cuts in front of me, my response is sometimes one of anger. But how do I feel when I'm the one in a hurry who wants to do the cutting?

Understanding, compassion, tolerance are all part of patience. By bearing calmly what we perceive as unwarranted trials, we exercise patience. When we refuse to complain even under provocation or strain, we exercise patience. When we remain steadfast and thoughtful, refusing to act or speak hastily, we exercise patience. If you can't muster up much, ask the Lord to show you all the ways He has had to be patient with you over the years.

During the reign of Queen Elizabeth I, a Dr. Thomas Cooper edited a scholarly dictionary. He spent eight years collecting materials for the addition of 33,000 words and other improvements. One day his wife went into the library. Under the pretense of fearing that he would kill himself with study, she burned every note he had made.

The doctor came in later, inquired who had done this, and his wife boldly answered that it was she. Dr. Cooper merely heaved a great sigh and said, "Oh, Dinah, Dinah, thou hast given me a world of trouble." Then he calmly sat down to another eight years of labor to replace what she had destroyed.

That's patience!

Misunderstanding of feminine jealousy. This blurb was discovered in the advertisement section of a newspaper: "Found—Lady's purse left in my car while parked. Owner can have same by describing property and paying for this ad. If owner can explain satisfactorily to my wife how purse got into car, will pay for ad myself."

That is a humorous sideline on an ancient problem. Eve is still counting Adam's ribs. As strange as it may seem, jealousy is an important and appropriate element of marriage. Even God says He gets jealous. But some husbands treat jealousy as a major drawback to the relationship.

What is godly jealousy? It is the desire to protect from interference a relationship that is precious and intimate. No husband or wife should stand by and let a third party intrude on the intimacy that is reserved for them alone.

To be sure, unhealthy possessiveness can stifle a relationship. But if your wife does act threatened when a pretty lady goes by, you need to ask yourself, "Am I making her feel secure in our relationship?" Your wandering eyes may tell her a story you wish she would not understand. Or your flirtatiousness could be killing both of you. One husband I know continually flirts with waitresses when he and his wife go out to eat. It is not only demeaning to their relationship, it is foolish.

While husbands can react with bitterness if their wives confront them, they need to watch their responses. She may be pointing out a deeper problem that he needs to deal with scripturally. Why? Because these kinds of behavior will inevitably lead to bitterness, if not divorce. Such husbands must examine themselves and work to change through the power and grace of God.

What a Husband Does When He's Embittered

Such things produce bitterness. But how can a husband or wife tell when he has become embittered? Temperaments vary the responses, but some of these types of behavior can be evidence of an underlying root of bitterness:

* Withdrawal
* Depression
* Revenge games
* Sarcastic comments
* Discourtesy
* Outbursts of anger
* The silent treatment
* Threats
* Less and less time in the home
* Drunkenness
* Put-downs
* Laziness
* Complaining
* Hypochondria
* Constant weariness
* Boredom
* Lack of interest in spiritual things
* Fantasies

On that last note—fantasies—it is amazing how our minds can flit off into a mental sequence of imagined revenge. Have you ever had a co-worker do something to you? What thoughts go through your mind? If you are like me, they are not only not nice, but often downright nasty, even murderous!

Or what about when we have a disagreement with our wife and fantasize about all the things we would like to do to her? One fellow told me how, after a vigorous confrontation with his wife, he slammed the door and stalked out of the house to sit in his car. There, he imagined all the things he wished he could do to her. He saw himself jetting to Boulder, Colorado, living under an assumed name. He pictured his wife living in abject poverty in a dump and wishing every day she hadn't hurt him. He even took it so far as to picture himself coming back ten years later and her weeping, saying she was wrong, all wrong. He then pictured himself falling on the stoop, dead, with her in anguish because she had caused all this pain. Finally, though, he came to his senses, realized it was stupid to be sitting out in the cold car when it was toasty inside, and he went back in to apologize for his foolish behavior.

How wasteful! Spending time in such fantasies is not only fruitless, but it reveals a husband who is not dealing with the real problem. How does one overcome a problem of bitterness in a marriage, especially when your wife is not helping?

Overcoming Bitterness

Let me offer several principles I have put to practice in my own marriage.

First, *learn to express your true feelings.*

One of the most difficult things for me to do early in our marriage was to tell my wife how I really felt about something—anything. "Would you like to go to the mall?" she would ask. My response: "What would *you* like to do?" Sometimes I was afraid to say what I wanted, or how I felt, or what to do about a problem because we might disagree.

In reality, I have discovered that while expressing my true feelings does not always avoid a disagreement, it goes a long way toward true openness, honesty, and integrity. Real communication flows. The channels open. The glut and smut of anger washes away in the wake of the cleansing wave of truth.

A happy marriage should be built solidly on truth, not pretense, lies, evasion, and sham. That means truth-telling to one another. After all, if we cannot tell the truth to our spouses, to whom can we tell it?

On the other hand, there are those husbands who seem to have no problem expressing their feelings. They are confident. They give the order and expect a salute without a whimper and a step-to without a stumble. Such men may need some lessons in tact and gentleness, but I think they may also be hiding behind their autocratic style. They are not expressing their real feelings either. It only appears that they do. Rather, they hide their vulnerability in volume and unquestioned obedience.

Second, *follow the principles of submission regardless of your wife's reactions.*

This principle has been emphasized several times in this book, but let me say it again: you are responsible to submit to Christ whether your wife does or not. God will not call you to account for her lack of submission but for yours. Obedience is not an option nor does it hinge on someone else's reaction.

Even if your wife is difficult, do not give up. As Paul said to the Galatians, "And let us not lose heart in doing good, for in due time we shall reap if we do not grow weary" (6:9).

Third, *take the problems one by one and deal with them.* I find that Satan loves to take a cloud of problems and turn it into a thunderhead. If he can huff and puff that situation into a storm in your mind, he can confuse you. If he can confuse you, he can win because God is not the author of confusion. The moment you find yourself becoming confused by problems, stop, think, and start writing them down. Just what is it that bothers you?

If you can make a list, you can do something about it. But as long as Satan keeps us from pinpointing the real difficulties, he can keep us from seeing the end of the storm.

I find that if I am experiencing the symptoms of bitterness, I need to sit down and clarify my thoughts by writing them out. This does several things. First, it forces me to articulate what I am feeling. Second, it lays out the whole scenario clearly. Third, it shows me the extent of what I am facing. I can know if I am dealing with one or ten thousand problems. When you get it all down in black and white, you see exactly who and what you are up against. It is much easier, then, to deal with the known rather than the imagined.

Fourth, *refuse to give in to anger.* Anger is not sin. It is the way you express anger that becomes sin. Refuse to let your anger so control you that you commit wrongs against God, your family, or yourself.

A truth my wife and I live by now is found in Proverbs 15:1: "A gentle answer turns away wrath, but a harsh word stirs up anger." Both my wife and I have learned that when one is angry, if the other can simply stay calm and not add some explosives of his own, things will always turn out right. It is when the calm one gives in to anger as well that greater problems result.

Fifth, *seek relief and help from God.* It is an amazing thing, but when you ask God for help, He comes through. Not always on our timetable, but definitely on His. Hebrews 4:16 tells us, "Let us therefore draw near with confidence to the throne of grace, that we may receive mercy and may find grace to help in time of need."

One of the greatest insights came to me some years ago about the nature of the "throne of grace." Has it ever occurred to you that when you pray, you have spiritually entered the throne room of God? Regardless of your surroundings, when you lift your heart to heaven you are transported to the very seat of heavenly government. Simply by prayer, either verbally or from the heart, we stand in the Father's very court. Immediately in conversation with the Creator of the universe. Now that is power.

Do you make use of that power? When you are in trouble? In need? Hurt? Angry? Bitter? Confused? If, when I am about to lose my calm about something, I have the presence of mind to stop and pray, I can usually turn the situation around. In fact, I even find myself praying that God would *remind* me to pray when a problem arises.

Sixth, *depend on God to meet your needs.* It is one thing to pray. It is another to expect God to do something. But the joy of Christianity is that, even if you doubt, and you are not sure what God will do, He answers. He *will* meet your needs. He will cleanse your heart of bitterness and anger and free you from the poison that corrodes the soul.

Ivan Turgenev once said, "I would give up all my genius, and all my books, if there were only some woman, somewhere, who cared whether or not I came home late for dinner."

I suspect that in every male heart there lies that longing. For those who have found a home for their heart, there is endless joy. But for those who lurk day by day in the squalor of bitterness, there is never a feast or a celebration. All is gray, and twilight comes soon.

May each of us who has chosen the route of marriage find the joy.

SECTION THREE:
HOW

—12—

How to Become a Submissive Man

Important questions any husband or wife who reads this book will ask are, "How do I become the kind of person you're talking about—a man in submission to Christ?" "How can I help my husband become this kind of man?" "How do I overcome my basic selfishness?" "How do we keep it all in balance?" How? *How?* HOW?

It is a lifetime project with ups, downs, and arounds. Being submissive to Christ requires becoming like Christ. It is a process, a never-ending process. No one arrives in this life. Only when we see Christ will we be totally like Him (I John 3:2).

Various Kinds of Submission

But one way to start is to consider that there are several kinds of submission evident in our world.

For instance, there are those who *do not submit at all.* Jesus's parable of the wicked husbandmen tells that story (Matthew 21:33-46). They rejected, beat up, and killed all of God's emissaries. These people refuse to recognize their Lord and Savior.

Then there are those who submit *reluctantly.* The parable of the friend who bangs on his neighbor's door at midnight until he gets him to rise demonstrates this kind of person.

After that are those who submit *selfishly.* They are willing to go along because of what they get out of it. The unrighteous judge only gave in to the poor woman seeking justice because she would wear him out otherwise (Luke 18:1-8). The selfish submitter is not really submitting at all. He is just looking out for number one.

Next are those who submit *expectantly.* These fellows are not all bad, but they submit out of an expectation of reward. They know submission will get them something. It is not selfish because they see that such submission is good for them and for others. They see it as beneficial for everyone concerned. The five virgins who kept their lamps trimmed may fall into this category (Matthew 25:1-13).

Then some submit *joyfully and eagerly.* They do so simply out of the joy and value of serving Jesus Christ. They not only see submission as a good, beneficial thing, but also as a jubilant thing. I think the parable of the talents in Matthew 25 pictures this type of person.

Finally, there are those who submit *sacrificially.* They do so out of love for Christ and simply because it is right to submit. Even if they do not have feelings of joy about doing so, they obey because He is worthy of obedience and love. The Samaritan in Luke 10 is one of these.

The question is: Which type of submission characterizes you?

Real submission involves all three of the latter qualities: a sense of expectation that there is a reward, a joy and eagerness about it because there is joy in serving Christ, and a sacrificial element. George Matheson once observed that "to lie down in a time of grief, to be quiet under the stroke of adversity, implies a great faith; but nothing requires greater strength than to work—to have a heavy weight in our heart and still to run the race; to have anguish in our spirit and still perform our daily tasks." That is the picture of sacrificial submission—the person who submits and continues to submit even when his own heart cries out in pain.

The Rightness Of It

Once you decide that you want to be a submissive man, the place to start is to *recognize the rightness of submission to Christ.*

In Luke 5:1-11, Jesus is at the Sea of Galilee and sees Simon Peter washing his net by his boat. He borrows the boat for awhile and addresses the crowd. After His message, He turns to Simon and instructs him to put the boat out into the deeper water and let down the nets for a catch. Simon's answer is interesting. He replies, "Master, we worked hard all night and caught nothing, but at Your bidding I will let down the nets." Simon is a fisherman. He has been at it all his life, and also all last night. He knows the fish are not netting today.

On the other hand, Jesus is a carpenter. He has met Simon on at least two previous occasions. At their first meeting, Jesus gave him the nickname, Peter or "Rock." Peter's brother Andrew is already convinced Jesus is the Messiah. And Jesus has already issued one invitation to both to follow Him. He will make them "fishers of men." Obviously, Simon is intrigued.

Now Jesus is telling him to go catch some fish.

Naturally, Simon has to inform Jesus of the facts—"we worked hard all night and caught nothing." It is like a disclaimer. "I don't want you to be embarrassed about this, Lord. I know you're the Messiah and all, but your vocation was in carpentry. So I'm just warning you, we shouldn't expect much."

But at the same time, he offers a good reason for obeying. "But at *Your* bidding I will let down the nets." In other words, "For anyone else, Lord, this would be ludicrous. But since it's you, I'll play along. Maybe we'll get lucky."

Simon didn't expect much, but he submitted. He recognized that it was right to obey Jesus simply because Jesus was Jesus.

Later, when the fish jammed his net and nearly sank his boat, Simon fell at Jesus' feet, crying, "Depart from me, for I am a sinful man, O Lord!" Obviously, Simon felt much more than a twinge of guilt about his earlier statement. He saw that Jesus had been gracious to him, and he did not deserve it.

In another context, Jesus said to His disciples, "Why do you call Me, 'Lord, Lord,' and do not do what I say?" (Luke 6:46). It is a contradiction to call Jesus, "Lord," and not obey Him. Strangely, it is Peter who later makes one of the most contradictory utterances of Scripture. In Acts 10:9-16 Peter receives a vision in which he is commanded to kill and eat certain "unclean" foods which no devout Jew would eat under the law. Peter replies, "By no means, Lord . . . " (Acts 10:14). Those two expressions cannot co-exist. It is either, "Yes, I will, *Lord.*" Or, "No, I won't, mere man."

If Jesus is Lord, then submission to Him is *right.* It is expected. There is no other way the universe—or an individual life—can function harmoniously.

By "right," there are certain things not meant. For one, submission is not simply the *expedient* thing to do. "Grit your teeth and accept it, Bud, if you want to be happy." Nor is it just the *decent* thing to do, as though we are granting Jesus a favor. Neither is it the *passable* thing to do, as though we are saying, "How little can I pay and still be accepted?"

No, a husband must say to himself and God, "I do this because it is the God-honoring thing to do, the righteous and godly thing to do."

It was quite a revelation to me in my Christian life when I began to see the beauty of doing things because they were right. For several years into my marriage, I practiced certain disciplines and performed certain deeds because it was fun. It was a joy to help my wife wash the dishes. It was fun to paint a room together. It was like the splendor of the mountain freshet, rushing and tumbling down the mountainside, full of life, glitter, and spray.

Then there came a time when the feelings wore off, and I began to do things from a sense of duty. It was sheer marital legalism. I took out the trash, but please don't expect me to smile. I cleaned up the basement, but don't push your luck on the attic! This was the mountain stream turned to a polluted brook. No burbling here. Just dead fish and dead nerves.

After that came a period of re-evaluation. What had happened to the joy? I began to ask myself why I did what I did. It occurred to me that there was a much better reason to do good to and for my wife: because I loved her and God. Put another way, because it was right.

I say that because too often we confuse love with a feeling. But love is an action, a choice, motivated by truth and holiness or rightness. When your life becomes filled and motivated by love and truth, a whole new perspective prevails, filtering everything. Suddenly you see things through the lens of Scripture. When you reach this point, all the joy, good feelings and peace flows back, but this time with the gentle curl of a hearty river that goes somewhere.

The Joy of Submission

That leads to a second principle: *Recognize the joy of submission.*

Remember the faithful slave who received five talents and went out and made five more (Matthew 25:20)? I get the idea that when his master returned and asked for a report, the slave bubbled over. "Master, you entrusted five talents to me; see, I have made five more talents." He couldn't wait for the Master to return. It was show-and-tell time.

Isn't that what submission to Christ does? You know He is with you; He loves you, and He is leading you to glory. Can anything less than real joy come from that?

Acts 5:12-42 has always thrilled me. Here Peter and John appear before the Sanhedrin to explain how they escaped from prison the night before, and why they continued to teach about Jesus. They are confronted about their teaching and Peter responds in his usual blunt way: "We must obey God rather than men." Then he goes on with a brief gospel presentation that cuts them all to the heart. They decide to dispose of these heretics when Gamaliel makes a speech that changes their minds.

Now they want to scourge them. That is thirty-nine lashes with a three-lashed whip which usually flayed a man's flesh to pulp.

You would think Peter and John would apply for new jobs after this, but Luke records their response in Acts 5:41: "So they went on their way from the presence of the Council, rejoicing that they had been considered worthy to suffer shame for His name." May God grant us all such joy when we suffer for Him!

That is marvelous, yet, it is the kind of response only a man in submission to Christ can give. One who obeys Him will live his days in joy.

That kind of attitude should bring an about-face in any Christian life. Obedience to Christ produces a crown of happiness far greater than any self-centered passion can.

The Results of Submission

But that brings up a third thought: *recognize the results of submission.*

Besides joy, all the rest of the fruit of the Spirit can penetrate into and flow out of our hearts. That is love, peace, patience, kindness, goodness, faithfulness, gentleness, self-control. Paul says it simply, " . . . walk by the Spirit, and you will not carry out the desire of the flesh" (Galatians 5:16).

It is fascinating to me to consult the *Times* bestseller list each week. I find that there are always several types of novels and books on it. First, there is usually a diet book. Then a seamy novel. After that, a health and exercise book. Next, some sort of positive thinking tome that promises good feelings for all. Usually there is something about success. After that a few spy novels or war thrillers. But what are they all selling? Self-control? Joy? Peace? Of a sort. They all try to produce a facsimile fruit for the spirit.

What startles me is that you can look at the list from any given year, and you will find the same types of books. Why? Because people discover that last year's books really did not work! They were not enough. They did not produce lasting results. So someone else comes out with a new gimmick.

But the answer is submission to Christ, not a new book.

Galatians 6:9 gives us another result. "And let us not lose heart in doing good, for in due time we shall reap if we do not grow weary." God's promise is that if you remain faithful to Him, you *will reap.* Payday is coming.

John suggests a third result in I John 2:28: "And now, little children, abide in Him, so that when He appears, we may have confidence and not shrink away from Him in shame at His coming."

There is an important truth in this verse. What if you are committing sin when Christ comes back, and you are ashamed to see Him? More than that, regardless of what you are doing when He comes, what if your whole life is one of shame? What if all you did was rebel and resist and fight Him daily?

True submission avoids that possibility. Your life pleases Him. There will be no shame. Rather, you exhibit a bold and holy confidence about the future.

A Consistent Spiritual Life

A fourth principle in helping us become submissive husbands is this: *cultivate a rigorous spiritual life.*

How are you conducting the spiritual side of your Christian life? What key elements are present? Is there prayer, Bible reading, memorization, application, study, sharing the faith, use of spiritual gifts in the church, giving, control of the tongue and thought-life?

These are only the beginning. They are the basics of spiritual life and discipline. There is nothing heaven-shattering about them. Yet, for some reason, many Christian men fail in these areas. They spend years resolving to have a regular Quiet Time. Yet, they cannot get down to Bible study. They try memorizing verses for a month. But, somehow, things just slide away. There is no spiritual impact on the wife or kids. Their leadership ranks down there with Caspar Milquetoast. They spend hours going to seminars, reading the right books, and crying out to God, "Help me get this together! *Please!*" but He doesn't seem to hear.

What do you do?

Harry Ironside, a noted theologian and teacher, lived a disciplined Christian life before his students. One of them came to him and asked him how he got up so early each morning. Ironside replied, "I set the alarm, and when it goes off, I get up." The student was amazed. He thought there must be some heaven-sent special power that helped him roll out of bed.

W. Somerset Maugham was asked how he produced so many fine books in his lifetime. He answered, "Every day I do two distasteful things. First, I get up in the morning. Second, I go to bed at night."

Spiritual disciplines are a matter of self-discipline. You take responsibility for yourself and do it. Yes, you pray for God's help. Yes, you enlist the aid of others, if that is possible. But it ultimately comes down to you. Will you or won't you? To get up or not to get up? To read the Bible or not to read? To pray or not to pray? Those are the questions.

For years I searched for some magical trick that would make my spiritual life—from personal disciplines to family instruction to husband-wife relations—easy. I have concluded that there isn't one. Why? Because each of us has three enemies doing everything they can to stop us—the world, the flesh, and the devil (I John 2:14-16). These spiritual distractions fill our eyes, hearts, and minds with problems and longings, planting doubts in our hearts. Anything to divert us from the important business of life. Anything to stop us, make us give up, detain us, help us procrastinate. Anything!

If you have had difficulty getting your spiritual life together, welcome to the moat. It's wet. It's muddy. And there are sharks in it, too. But God's grace is greater. Depend on Him for all your needs, then go out and do all you can with all you have. Don't try to figure out where you end and He begins. Just walk with Him. " . . . Greater is He who is in you . . . . " Start with one thing and add. As each element becomes a part of your life-pattern, you'll see Him change it, develop it, build it, and perfect it day by day, year by year. One of the most exciting things about being a Christian is not that we have a great life, but that we have a great Lord who comes right into our lives.

Persevere Despite Setbacks

Here's a fifth thought: *Persevere.*

Chuck Swindoll's book *Three Steps Forward, Two Steps Back* describes the process. Sometimes you advance fast. Sometimes slowly. Sometimes you are driven back, and you watch all you thought you had accomplished blow by. But God is taking us someplace, and we can be sure He will get us there. "For I am confident of this very thing, that He who began a good work in you will perfect it until the day of Christ Jesus" (Philippians 1:6). We must continue applying the principles of God's Word even when it looks like evil is winning.

One of my favorite characters in Scripture is Habakkuk. He looked around at the Judah of 650 B.C. and cried out to God, "What's happening, Lord? All I see is evil, evil everywhere. Murder, strife, robbery, you name it. What are you doing?"

God tells him, "It's not the way it looks, Habakkuk. In fact, I am doing something. I'm raising up an army—the Babylonians. They're going to gallop in and trample Judah into the dirt."

Habakkuk drops his jaw. "Hold it, Lord! You're holy. How can You support people like that?"

God answers with a number of woes—judgments on evil people. Basically He says that anyone and everyone who commits sin will be punished.

At that point, God's revelation ends. But Habakkuk is just starting. In chapter three, he writes one of the awesome psalms of Scripture that praises, rejoices in, and extols God for His majesty, justice, perfection, and power. He asks God to be merciful to his sinful countrymen, but at the same time he is utterly confident. He ends up saying, *"Though the fig tree should not blossom, and there be no fruit on the vines, though the yield of the olive should fail, and the fields produce no food, though the flock should be cut off from the fold, and there be no cattle in the stalls, yet I will exult in the Lord, I will rejoice in the God of my salvation. The Lord God is my strength, and He has made my feet like hind's feet, and makes me walk on my high places"* (Habakkuk 3:17-19).

What was Habakkuk saying? "No matter what happens, God, no matter how bad it gets, I'm going to trust you. I'm going to praise you. I will rejoice in *you!* you're the source of my strength, and you've changed me from being a cowering prophet into one who prances like a mountain deer on the towering places of the world."

I remember when I memorized that last verse. The next week everything went wrong! It was like the Lord was trying to determine if I really believed it! So I muscled it through. And found out it worked. It was true. I could rejoice in God even when things became rough.

Try this attitude: whenever any trial comes to your marriage, thank God, because you know He is managing your life, and this is one more element of His perfection program. He believes enough in your marriage to help make you and your wife a little more like Jesus through it.

Give God Time, Too

One last principle: *Give God time to work, too.*

Peter Marshall wrote some wonderful sermons in his day. One illustration that struck me was about a little boy who brings his father a broken toy. Dad sets about fixing it, and the boy watches. But it seems to take longer and longer, and finally, in frustration, the boy snatches the toy out of Dad's hand, crying, "I knew you couldn't do it." Marshall then makes the application that when we pray, we put our broken "toys" into God's hands. But we need to let Him fix them on His time schedule, not ours.

Don't snatch things out of God's hands. Do what you should do, but be patient. God is not finished with you, your wife, or anyone else yet.

—13—

For Wives Only: When Your Husband Doesn't Obey Christ

Somehow I suspect that more wives will buy this book than husbands. I hope it does get into the hands and hearts of many men. But I think it is appropriate to address the ladies who will read this book.

First, let me salute you. As an old saying goes: Just remember the Pilgrim Mothers. They not only had to put up with everything the Pilgrim Fathers had to put up with, but they also had to put up with the Pilgrim Fathers!

You wives have put up with a lot in your days. I suspect that some of you are crying for a little help. "It's the impossible dream, Mark. My husband would never take this to heart." I hope that is not true. Just the same, there is no reason for despair. Scripture has a fine-tuned word for all those women out there with disobedient husbands. I Peter 3:1-6.

In the same way, you wives, be submissive to your own husbands so that even if any of them are disobedient to the word, they may be won without a word by the behavior of their wives, as they observe your chaste and respectful behavior. And let not your adornment be external only—braiding the hair, and wearing gold jewelry, or putting on dresses; but let it be the hidden person of the heart, with the imperishable quality of a gentle and quiet spirit, which is precious in the sight of God. For in this way in former times the holy women also, who hoped in God, used to adorn themselves, being submissive to their own husbands. Thus Sarah obeyed Abraham, calling him lord, and you have become her children if you do what is right without being frightened by any fear.

Not Just About Unsaved Husbands

This passage is often interpreted as relating to wives with unsaved husbands. Certainly it applies in that area. But Peter says, "So that even if any of them are *disobedient* to the word . . . ." That includes any husband, even a Christian, who disobeys God's word. In fact, it may be written expressly to wives with Christian husbands who are rebellious and flout scriptural truths. Just because a man is born again does not mean he is walking in the Spirit.

What then is Peter's admonition?

Peter is thinking of submission. He has gone through the numerous relationships of life and applied the principles of submission to each. Now he has reached wives. What docs hc say?

Be Submissive

Peter's first order is that the wives "be submissive." It is the same military term used elsewhere to mean "be subject, be under the authority of." Such submission does not mean . . .

-you're a doormat
-you're inferior
-you never participate in the decision-making process
-your husband is always right
-his word is your command
-you never express your opinion
-you keep quiet and obey without question
-he always wins
-you're consigned to a life of slavery
-he's the captain and you're the private

Real submission is a matter of the heart before Christ first, and then as a godly response to your husband's authority. It means your husband has a rightful place as head of your home. It means that God holds *him* accountable for family decisions. It means you are accountable to God *and* him. It means that when it comes to a final decision involving his authority, *he* must make it. It means that you should not try to usurp his position by any means—for there will be divine consequences.

When you repeated your marriage vows, you willingly and voluntarily placed yourself under his authority. Why did you do that? Because you wanted it, longed for it, dreamed about it. Has it turned out as you thought? Has *he* turned out as you imagined?

Probably not. Marriage is like starting a campfire. When first ignited, with all the paper and trimmings, it flames up and roars. Everyone stands back in amazement. The first passions seem inextinguishable. But then it settles down. And sometimes nearly goes out! You begin fanning the few remaining coals. If they are from the right sort of wood, dry and hard, eventually they do burn brightly. A real, gentle, hot fire which is good for cooking and watching develops. And lasts. A new kind of passion soars. You enter into the true "bliss" of marriage.

But it does not always happen. The wife refuses to submit. The husband lashes out and crushes her down. She becomes a feminist. He becomes a chauvinist. They retire to their corners until a bell rings and again they come out fighting. A long feud sets in.

That is when the question proposes itself: Will you volunteer to submit again—even if he remains mean and incorrigible? Will you honor your vows?

The Expression of Submission

Peter provides us with several elements of the wife's submission. He defines it in three areas.

1. *Silence in spiritual things.* Notice that Peter says that the husbands "may be won *without a word* by the behavior of their wives . . . ." A husband will be more receptive to the gospel if his wife goes about her business as a wife and does not constantly badger him into attending church or being the spiritual leader.

That is difficult. We Christians are a wordy bunch. We share. We pray. We testify. We witness. We preach. But words often count for little in the eyes of the unbelieving, or the doubting, or the disobedient. They want to see deeds, action, behavior, change. Right words are easy. Right conduct is tough.

Does this mean the wife never says a thing?

Peter's point is that the wife emphasizes conduct. She does not preach at him, nag, complain, put him down, examine, judge, debate. Rather, she takes action. She treats him with honor. She serves him good meals. She does the housework with a smile. She gives *him* her best.

Peter is also emphasizing the spiritual element of her talk. Peter's admonition is, "Stop beating him with the Word, wives, and go practice the Word. That will make your husbands stand up and take notice."

I remember reading a story about a wife who decided to let her life do the talking. She stopped haranguing her husband about his lack of spirituality and threw herself into walking in the Spirit. For two weeks he didn't say a word. The pressure was building inside her. Finally, in frustration, she exploded. "I've made some big changes around here, and you haven't said a word." He answered, "You've made two week changes before. I'm waiting to see if it's permanent."

I have read about wives who could cook up fantastic desserts—for the church socials—but their husbands never tasted them in the daily round of meals. I have heard of wives who did everything for everyone—except dear old Hubby. But Peter is saying, "Reverse gears, ladies. Take church out of drive and put your home into gear. That will make him take note."

I want to encourage you, ladies. Multitudes of men have been won by godly wives—both to the Lord and to His Lordship. Don't despair. Don't resort to useless, worldly tactics. Take Peter's admonition to heart. It works if you choose to work with it.

2. *Chaste.* What kind of behavior is Peter suggesting? Chastity, first. The word means to be "pure, innocent." It is much more than sexual purity. It has to do with your whole lifestyle.

Occasionally I meet women who seem to know too much. They are hard. They act tough. They have lost their innocence. They have tried everything—sex, drugs, alcohol, you name it. There is nothing fresh and vital about them. It is as though all the goodness has drained away. They use foul language. Their eyes seem to see more than just what is there, and their faces show it by their knowing leers. Frequent sexual innuendoes spot their speech. They are simply not chaste people.

Christian wives can fall into this in a much subtler way. They give in to gossip. They indulge their fantasies in television and secular novels. They drink—often in secret. They dream about other men. They fantasize. They may not commit adultery with their bodies. But they are not chaste. There is a callousness, a brazenness about them. Somehow the softness has disappeared.

A woman who is chaste protects her innocence. She does not go in the way of temptation, and she keeps herself free of sin. She keeps short accounts with the Lord. She has eyes for only one man—her man.

Some women today try to say, "Men don't want virgins anymore; they want experienced women."

I disagree. Men do want soft, kind, loving, pure, innocent wives, not women of the world. Maybe not all of them. But perhaps the men who want something else are not worth wanting.

3. *Be respectful.* Peter says that a man is won by your "chaste and *respectful* behavior." Respect is something a man needs. Perhaps more than any other gift a wife might give, this one ranks highest.

Do you respect your husband?

Or do you talk about his weaknesses, foibles, and failings to your friends and neighbors like he was the proverbial dog?

When you speak to him, do you lash him with put-downs, gripes, complaints, undermining his confidence and self-esteem? Or do you show respect and deference, understanding that he is not perfect? One wife repeatedly referred to her husband in conversation as "that idiot I'm married to." I understand his reluctance to go out in public with her on his arm.

Do you make demands on your husband that he cannot possibly meet? One wife's husband made over seventy thousand dollars a year. But she was angry because she felt he ought to go into his own business and "really make some money." She nagged him about it all the time. What he made was just not enough. This wife was not only being unreasonable, but unrealistic, greedy, materialistic, and demeaning to her husband's provision.

Do you treat him like a child—correcting him, chiding him, cutting him down in front of others?

How do you respond when he tells you his dreams, his hopes? With kind support, or with a harsh comment: "You'll never do that!"

How do you act when he bares his heart to you, with gentle love or a sarcastic snort?

In seminary, Dr. Howard Hendricks once showed a film clip in which a husband tells his wife about a possible promotion at work. The scene unfolds as they are getting ready for bed. He goes on and on enthusiastically. Meanwhile, the wife settles herself down, turns to the wall, and starts snoring. I remember thinking at the time that I would never want to be married to a woman who treated me like that.

Marabel Morgan has some good advice in her book, *Total Woman* (which I read as a single guy, figuring this was what I needed to look for).

Accept him.

Appreciate him.

Admire him.

Unfortunately, many men in the business world have few, if any, who treat them like they matter. During my years as a college student, I worked in a box factory each summer. I was often amazed at how those workers were treated by the foremen and managers—like they were dolts, fools, incompetents, and shiftless. Engineers would come out with stopwatches, write on their sheets of paper, and move on without a friendly word to the machine operators. Managers would curse and yell at workers for the slightest infractions. It was war. If men get the same treatment at home, it is little wonder that they have no relish for going there.

Be Supportive

The second primary area Peter mentions is being supportive. He says, "And let not your adornment be external only—braiding the hair, and wearing gold jewelry, and putting on dresses; but let it be the hidden person of the heart, with the imperishable quality of a gentle and quiet spirit, which is precious in the sight of God."

Look your best physically

Dr. Willard F. Harley has recently published a book about the needs of men and women in marriage (*His Needs, Her Needs: Building An Affair-Proof Marriage*). He mentions that one of the husband's primary needs is to feel that his wife is attractive. Husbands do want their wives to look good. He wants to feel that pride of association when they go out in public together.

When Peter says a wife is not to "braid her hair, wear gold jewelry or put on dresses," he is not saying a wife should not seek to look nice. He is simply putting his emphasis on the spiritual side of things. Look your best physically, ladies, but make spiritual matters your primary concern.

Look your best spiritually

Peter mentions two characteristics in this passage: gentleness and quietness.

Gentle. It's that "gentle" spirit which husbands notice. The word means humble, considerate, courteous, meek. She does not come across as a know-it-all or a nag. She does not push. She is willing to wait on God. And her husband.

Gentleness is the ability to keep great physical power and anger under control, even under the most trying conditions.

A friend of mine came home one night irritated about a rough day at work. When he reached the kitchen door, his wife made a comment about his appearance. In anger he tore off his watch and threw it at the wall. Now, at that moment, his wife could have added fuel to his anger by abandoning any semblance of gentleness. But with great ease and calm, she simply leaned down, picked up the watch, listened, shook her head with a smile, and said, "Takes a licking, but keeps on ticking!" Both of them suddenly convulsed with laughter. Her gentleness turned a tense situation into a memorable anecdote.

Quiet. The second quality is quietness. Second Thessalonians 3:11-13, I Peter 4:14-15, and I Timothy 5:13 reflect that this quietness also relates to gossip. A woman is not to be a busybody or argumentative.

To be the wife of a happy man, women need to give their husbands quiet in their homes. While a primary need of the wife is talk and conversation with her husband, sometimes a man needs space, breathing room, a chance to bask in the quiet. It is a balance point each couple needs to find.

Be Steadfast

The third major element of Peter's admonition to wives with disobedient husbands is to be steadfast. Hang in there. Don't give up. Peter says, "Thus Sarah obeyed Abraham, calling him lord, and you have become her children if you do what is right without being frightened by any fear."

Two thoughts.

1. *Hope.* Trust God to work in and with your husband. Don't give up on your marriage, your husband, or your God.

2. *Do not fear.* Continue to do what is right even if he doesn't seem to notice or care.

Remember: your submission is not a means to manipulate your husband into doing what you want. It is not a weapon. Rather, you submit to him, love him, are chaste, respectful, gentle, and quiet *because it is right.* It pleases God. Your ultimate aim is to please *Him* first, and then him. If you please Jesus, the chances are you will eventually please your husband.

The Church Can Help

In the case of a husband who won't change, the church can be of practical assistance and encouragement to wives.

For one thing, the church can pray.

For another, the men in the congregation can go out of their way to befriend these husbands.

For a third, the church can seek to support these wives in any way possible. They have a tough challenge. It will never be easy. Most of all, the church and pastor can teach all of God's truth regarding submission—by sermon and example.

Finally

These commands are not just for wives with disobedient husbands, though. They are for all wives . . . and husbands.

Let me conclude this chapter and this book with two final illustrations about the quality of marriages.

Mstislav Rostropovich, famed conductor and orchestral genius, was asked on a talk show if it was true he had married his wife just four days after they met. He replied, "Regretfully, yes, I lost four days."

About three hundred years ago a man lost his job in a customs house. He went home, broken-hearted, to tell his wife Sophia. To his astonishment she only beamed at him. "Now you can write your book!" He answered, "Yes, and what will we live on while I'm writing?" Sophia quickly went to a drawer and took out a cache of money. "I've always known that you were a man of genius," she said. "I knew that someday you would write an immortal masterpiece. So every week out of the money you have given me for housekeeping, I have saved something. Here is enough to last us one whole year."

That amazed husband went to his study and began writing. His name was Nathaniel Hawthorne. His book was *The Scarlet Letter.*

It is my prayer that every husband and wife who reads this book will make a new commitment to work on the principles outlined in it, to discover the joy of mutual submission. Those wonderful women we chose to be our life's partners deserve our love, leadership, and loyalty.

Submission: The willing acceptance of another's authority. It's not just for wives. It's for husbands, too.

MARRIAGE

When God made light, the angels
drew near to let the refractions roll
over their faces like a symphony.

When God made earth, they poked
their fingers into its moistness;
they put a fleck to their nose and smiled.

When God made the sea, they kicked
at the foam and sat in its cool
till their bones laughed.

When God made a rose, they parted
its petals and passed it among
themselves, saying, "So fragile,
yet it grasps the soul like steel."

When God made a giraffe,
they touched the strange hide,
and murmured to themselves that God
was up to something magnificent.

When God made man, each one
retired to his chamber and peered
into the writings, looking for some
clue to the mystery.

When God made woman, they came
back out of their chambers and gazed,
their jaws slack with awe.

When God joined man to woman
and said, "Let them become one flesh,"
everything suddenly made sense.
The cheering still shakes the galaxies.

—Mark Littleton